THE FOOD WARS

THE FOOD WARS

Walden Bello

VERSO
London • New York

First published by Verso 2009
Copyright © Walden Bello 2009
All rights reserved

The moral rights of the author have been asserted

1 3 5 7 9 10 8 6 4 2

Verso
UK: 6 Meard Street, London W1F 0EG
US: 20 Jay Street, Suite 1010, Brooklyn, NY 11201
www.versobooks.com

Verso is the imprint of New Left Books

ISBN-13: 978-1-84467-331-5

British Library Cataloguing in Publication Data
A catalogue record for this book is available from the British Library

Library of Congress Cataloging-in-Publication Data
A catalog record for this book is available from the Library of Congress

Typeset by Hewer Text UK Ltd, Edinburgh
Printed in the United States by Maple Vail

To Scarlett
Venustas vestra vincit omnia

Contents

Acknowledgements

A number of colleagues and friends made this book possible with their help, their inspiration, their ideas, and their company.

Above all, I am indebted to Mara Baviera, who served as my research assistant and was largely responsible for Chapter Six ("Agrofuels and Food Insecurity").

Without Nicole Curato taking over some of my teaching tasks at the University of the Philippines and Sabrina Gacad assuming a number of my organizational responsibilities at the Freedom from Debt Coalition, this book would never have been finished.

Joy Chavez-Malaluan, coordinator of the Philippine program of Focus on the Global South, was very helpful during the different stages in the conceptualization and writing of this book. I also wish to thank my other colleagues in Focus and the Freedom from Debt Coalition for being very tolerant of the many instances I might have departed from comradely behavior as I struggled with the book.

This book is my way of saying thank you to all those who have helped me work through food and agriculture issues over the last three decades. Among them must be counted Frances Moore Lappé, Peter Rosset, Eric Holt-Gimenez, Anuradha Mittal, Ric Reyes, Jun Borras, Jenny Franco, Mary Ann Manahan, Marissa de Guzman, Kanjapat Korsieporn, Ging Gutierrez, Joe Collins, Marilyn Borchardt, Martha Katigbak, Mary Beth

Brangan, Philip McMichael, Harriet Friedmann, Raj Patel, Joel Rocamora, David O'Connor, Aileen Kwa, Marco Garrido, Annette Desmarais, Nettie Wiebe, Henry Saragih, Rafael Alegria, Isabelle Delforge, Robin Broad, Chanida Bamford, Shalmali Guttal, David Kinley, Indra Lubis, John Cavanagh, Vandana Shiva, Laura Carlsen, and Teddy Goldsmith.

Roane Carey inadvertently got this ball rolling when he asked me to write an article on the global food crisis for the *Nation*. Sebastian Budgen introduced me to Verso. Tariq Ali invited me to write the book. And Jake Stevens and Mark Martin helped me bring this project to completion.

Ed Rodriguez and Dick Ng were always there to provide good advice, good company, and good wine whenever I encountered an intellectual roadblock, of which there were many.

While I am very grateful to all these fine friends and colleagues, I must also say that none of them must be held responsible for any errors of fact and analysis this book may contain.

Walden Bello
Quezon City
Feb. 28, 2009

Introduction

FROM 2006 TO 2008, the prices of basic commodities spiraled, making essential foodstuffs unaffordable for vast numbers of people. International agencies were caught flat-footed, and the World Food Program warned that its rapidly diminishing stocks might not be able to deal with the emergency.

The surging cost of rice, wheat, and vegetable oils raised the food import bills of the least developed countries (LDCs) by 37 percent in 2008, from $17.9 million the previous year to $24.6 million. These increases followed a 30 percent increase in 2006. By the end of 2008, the United Nations reported that "the annual food import basket in LDCs cost more than three times that of 2000, not because of the increased volume of food imports, but as the result of rising food prices."[1] These tumultuous developments added 75 million people to the ranks of the hungry and drove an estimated 125 million into extreme poverty.[2]

Alarmed by massive global demand, countries like China and Argentina resorted to taxes or quotas on their rice and wheat exports to avert local shortages. Rice exports were simply banned in Cambodia, Egypt, India, Indonesia, and Vietnam. South-South solidarity crumbled in the crisis, a victim of collateral damage.

Food shortages had become a global reality.

Global Crisis, Global Protests

Where civil society was fragile, the food crisis had an incendiary effect. Some thirty countries experienced violent popular actions in 2007 and 2008, among them Bangladesh, Burkina Faso, Cameroon, Côte d'Ivoire, Egypt, Guinea, India, Indonesia, Mauritania, Mexico, Morocco, Mozambique, Senegal, Somalia, Uzbekistan, and Yemen. Across the continents, people came out in the thousands to protest the uncontrolled rise in the price of imported staple goods. Scores of people died in these demonstrations of popular anger.

Impact of high food prices by region
(additional number of undernourished in 2007)

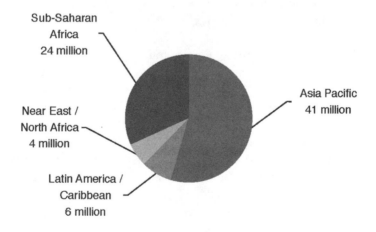

Source:
Food and Agriculture Organization,
"Briefing Paper: Hunger on the Rise" (2009)

Typical of the dynamics of these actions were events in Senegal. There the state imported up to 80 percent of its rice, making it particularly vulnerable to global price instability. In April 2008, responding to domestic criticism, President

Abdoulaye Wade announced a plan to increase rice production fivefold. But this failed to calm the growing unrest. A week later, about a thousand Senegalese took to the streets.[3] The fate of the government hung on the availability of rice, a commodity that Senegal had once been able to produce in sufficient quantities to meet its needs.

The most dramatic developments, however, took place in Haiti, where 80 percent of the population was subsisting on less than two dollars a day. In the first four months of 2008, the price of rice doubled. The physical effects of the resultant shortages were so widespread and intense that, according to one account, the Haitians coined the phrase "Clorox hunger" to describe a pain "so torturous that people felt like their stomachs were being eaten away by bleach or battery acid."[4] Rioting spread through the country, ending only when the Senate fired the prime minister. In their intensity, the Haiti riots reminded observers of the anti–International Monetary Fund (IMF) riots in Venezuela—the so-called *caracazo*—almost two decades before, which reshaped the contours of that country's politics.

Number of undernourished people in the developing world (WFS target)

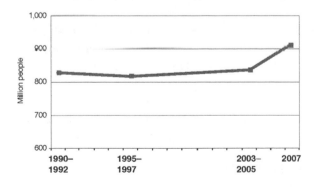

Source:
Food and Agriculture Organization,
"Briefing Paper: Hunger on the Rise" (2009)

A Perfect Storm

The international press and many academics proclaimed the end of the era of cheap food and traced the crisis to a variety of causes: the failure of poorer countries to develop their agricultural sectors; strains on the international food supply created by dietary changes among China's and India's expanding middle classes; speculation in commodity futures; the conversion of farmland into urban real estate; climate change; and the diversion of corn and sugarcane from food production to the production of agrofuels.

The United Nations report *World Economic Situation and Prospects* called the food shortage the product of a "perfect storm," or an explosive confluence of various developments. Speculative movements that brought about the global financial crisis beginning in the summer of 2007 were implicated. According to the United Nations, the impact on food prices of speculation by financial investors in commodities and commodity futures markets "has been considerable."

> Speculation in the actual, physical exchange of commodities certainly influenced prices as speculators bought and stored commodities, betting on price increases. Such positions have temporarily reduced the supply of goods and have no doubt affected price movements directly. The impact of speculation in futures markets (that is to say, where speculators do not physically trade any commodities) on price trends is much more difficult to determine, however. Futures trades are bets on buying or selling goods entitlements which are continuously rolled over. It is therefore not clear whether such trading does more to commodity prices other than increase their volatility.

It could, however, be argued that

> increased global liquidity and financial innovation has also led to increased speculation in commodity markets. Conversely,

the financial crisis contributed to the slide in commodity prices from mid-2008 as financial investors withdrew from commodity markets and, in addition, the United States dollar appreciated as part of the process of the deleveraging of financial institutions in the major economies.[5]

Others, such as Peter Wahl of the German advocacy organization WEED (World Economy, Ecology, and Development), were less uncertain, claiming that, in fact, speculation in agro-commodity futures was the key factor in the extraordinary rise in the prices of food commodities in 2007 and 2008. These analysts asserted that when the real estate bubble burst in 2007 and trade in mortgage-based securities and other derivatives started to collapse, hedge funds and other speculative agents moved into commodity futures, causing a sharp increase in trading and contracts accompanied by little or no increase in the production of agricultural commodities. It was this move into commodity futures for quick profits followed by a move out after the commodities bubble burst that triggered the 71 percent rise in the Food and Agriculture Organization (FAO) food price index during just fifteen months between the end of 2006 and March 2008, and its decline after July 2008.[6]

Speculation, along with the channeling of agricultural production to biofuel production—a development that will be examined in detail in Chapter 6—was certainly among the factors that created a "perfect storm" in 2006 to 2008. Yet long-term developments largely fostered this economic typhoon. In the years leading up to the sharp price rises of 2008, demand for basic grains—rice, wheat, barley, maize, and soybeans—exceeded production, with granary stores falling to 40 percent of their levels in 1998–99, and the stock-to-use ratio reaching record lows for total grains and multiyear lows for maize and vegetable oils.[7] The United Nations asserted that this woeful shortfall of supply was due to the degradation of the agricultural sectors of developing countries because of the "weakening [of]

Patterns of price developments among food commodities, 2003–July 2008

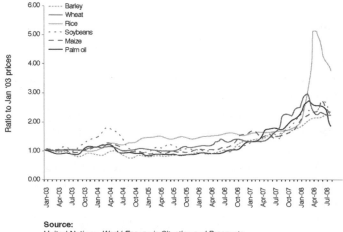

Source:
United Nations, *World Economic Situation and Prospects*
(New York: UN, 2009), p. 47.

investment and agricultural support measures" resulting in a condition in which "productivity growth for major food crops has stalled, and there has been no significant increase in the use of cultivated land."[8] It was clear that more than just the short-term factors of speculation and agrofuel production were at work. The FAO reported that "even before the recent surge in food prices, worrisome long-term trends towards increasing hunger were already apparent," with 848 million people suffering from chronic hunger in 2003–2005, an increase of 6 million from the 1990–92 figure of nearly 842 million.[9]

Certainly a vital, if not *the* central force behind the food price crisis of 2006 to 2008 was the massive agricultural policy reorientation known as "structural adjustment." This book will take a close look at that program, imposed by the World Bank and the International Monetary Fund on more than ninety developing and transitional economies over a twenty-year period beginning in the early 1980s.

Whatever the configuration of factors, the widespread pain did not go away when prices inched back down in the second half of 2008. According to the FAO, as of October 2008 there were still thirty-six countries in critical situations

> owing to exceptional supply shortfalls, general lack of access or severe localized food insecurity of displaced populations requiring immediate food assistance. Most of these countries have not seen their situation improve, and in some cases the situation has worsened because of persistent high prices, as food prices have been sticky on the downside and the dollar appreciation has offset some of the price effects of falling commodity prices.[10]

For the world's poor, high food prices had become a fact of life.

The Orthodox Account: A Critique

Perhaps the most influential orthodox view on the causes, dynamics, and solution to the food price crisis was provided by the Oxford University economist Paul Collier in an article that came out in *Foreign Affairs* in November of 2008. Collier, author of the controversial *The Bottom Billion*, asserted that the problems stemmed from the increased demand for food in Asia brought on by prosperity. He argued that supplies were lagging for three reasons: governments had failed to promote commercial farming, especially in Africa; the European Union had banned genetically modified organisms (GMOs); and the United States had diverted about a third of its grain to the production of ethanol instead of food.

In the 1980s and 1990s, it was widely acknowledged that the world had enough food to feed some seven or eight billion people and that hunger and malnutrition were due to unequal income and unequal access to food. By the turn of the millennium, the problem had indeed become one of production and supply constraints, but not quite in the ways Collier described. The diversion of corn to agrofuel production was certainly one incontrovertible cause, but the two other factors he identifies— the European ban on GMOs and the restraints placed on the growth of commercial agriculture—are questionable.

Collier's claim that Europe's GMO ban—now eased, incidentally—was a key constraint on production is disingenuous. Europe's main problem with its agricultural production has, in fact, been the overproduction and dumping arising from heavy subsidization. He deplored, though, the ban's impact on Africa's farmers, claiming that it discouraged them from exploiting genetically engineered agriculture out of fear their exports would be barred from entering Europe. Collier said a "New Green Revolution" based on genetic engineering (GE) is necessary in Africa, where agricultural productivity is low, because the continent missed the first such revolution, in the 1960s and 1970s.

Collier's attribution of Africa's agricultural problems to, more than anything else, the lack of a GE-inspired miracle is idiosyncratic, to say the least, and his dismissal of concerns about GMO-based agriculture is cavalier. He implied that criticism of the new genetic technology has no scientific basis, and failed to acknowledge the well-known negative ecological and social impacts of the first, chemical-intensive Green Revolution. Fears about GE are well grounded empirically, and proponents of GMOs have not been able to alleviate worries that transgenic foods may have unexpected reactions in humans. These new foods have not been selected for human consumption by eons of evolution, nor have they been rigorously tested in accordance with universally recognized precautionary principles. Their makers have failed to prove that nontarget populations will not be negatively affected by genetic modification aimed at specific pests, as in the case of Bt corn, which was genetically modified to resist the soil bacterium *Bacillus thuringiensis* but in addition killed the larvae of the monarch butterfly. Further, they have taken no steps to mitigate the very real threat to biodiversity posed by GMOs:

> The effects of transgenic crops on biodiversity far extend the concerns already raised by monocropping under the Green Revolution. Not only is diversity decreased through the physical loss of species, but because of its "live" aspect, [transgenic crops have] the potential to contaminate, and potentially to dominate, other strains of the same species. While this may be a limited concern with respect to the contamination of another commercial crop, it is significantly more worrisome when it could contaminate and eradicate generations of evolution of diverse and subtly differentiated strains of a single crop, such as the recently discovered transgenic contamination of landraces of indigenous corn in Mexico.[11]

Collier's advocacy of GE is, in fact, out of line with even orthodox expert opinion at this point. The recently released International Assessment of Agricultural Knowledge, Science, and Technology for Development (IAASTD)—sponsored and funded by, among others, United Nations agencies and the World Bank—failed to endorse GE crops, choosing instead to highlight the lingering doubts and uncertainties regarding their ecological and health impacts.[12]

Collier's promotion of an African Green Revolution powered by genetic engineering was linked to his third contention that the nondevelopment of commercial agriculture in Africa has been responsible for the failure of supply to keep up with continental demand. Instead, he wrote, "over the past 40 years, African governments have worked to scale back large commercial agriculture."[13] For Collier, the solution to Africa's food shortages are commercial agricultural farms employing genetically modified seeds. Peasant agriculture is not only less than ideal, it's part of the problem. Peasants, according to Collier, are not entrepreneurs or innovators, being too concerned with their food security. The people most capable of taking the role of innovative entrepreneur, he argued, are those involved in commercial farming operations:

> reluctant peasants are right: their mode of production is ill suited to modern agricultural production, in which scale is helpful. In modern agriculture, technology is fast-evolving, investment is lumpy, the private provision of transportation infrastructure is necessary to counter the lack of its public provision, consumer food chains are fast-changing and best met by integrated marketing chains, and regulatory standards are rising toward the holy grail of traceability of produce back to its source.[14]

Collier's account has, at least, the merit of posing a stark choice between peasant or small-farm-based agriculture and industrial agriculture as the solution to the world's food needs. However, his choice, the environmentally stressful Brazilian model of industrial agriculture, is not one that should elicit much enthusiasm from anyone. Moreover, the Brazilian agro-enterprise is part of a larger system of global industrial agriculture marked by large agribusiness combines, monopolistic trading companies, long-distance transportation of food, and supermarkets catering largely to the global elite and upper middle class. This globalized system of production has created severe strains on the environment, marginalized large numbers of people from the market, and contributed to greater poverty and greater income disparities within countries and globally. The Brazilian model is part of the problem, but the only indication that Collier is aware of the model's systemic flaws comes when he notes, "Some have criticized the Brazilian model for displacing peoples and destroying the rain forest, which has indeed happened in places where commercialism has gone unregulated."[15]

But what is most astounding in Collier's account is the absence of any reference to the externally imposed policies that have severely weakened agricultural capacity in a wide swath of developing countries and transitional economies. He notes that part of the problem in Africa has been the dismantling of publicly funded research stations, part of a "more widespread malfunctioning of the public sector." But he fails to point out that this breakdown was due to International Monetary Fund and World Bank structural adjustment policies that systematically starved agriculture of state support. In October 2008, a report by an independent evaluation team of the World Bank simply confirmed what others had been decrying for two decades:

> Bank policies in the 1980s and 1990s that pushed African governments to cut or eliminate fertilizer subsidies, decontrol prices and privatize may have improved fiscal discipline but did not accomplish much for food production, the evaluation said . . . It had been expected that higher prices for crops would give farmers an incentive to grow more, while competition among private traders reduced the costs of seeds and fertilizer. But those market forces often failed to work as hoped.[16]

The Brazilian model and structural adjustment went hand in hand. Both were central elements of a capitalist transformation of agriculture that was intended to integrate local food systems, via trade liberalization, into a global system marked by a division of labor that would allegedly result in greater efficiency and greater prosperity in the aggregate. Collier and other orthodox observers fail to see that structural adjustment policies were the cutting edge of this process of supplanting peasant producers with capitalist entrepreneurs producing for global markets. Structural adjustment was an indispensable step towards a large-scale globally integrated capitalist industrial agriculture.

Death of the Peasantry

In putting down peasants and small farmers, Collier is not alone. Many analysts, some of whom boast progressive credentials, share his views. In his acclaimed 1994 book *The Age of Extremes,* Eric Hobsbawm wrote that "the death of the peasantry" was "the most dramatic and far-reaching social change of the second half of this century," one that "cut us off forever from the world of the past."[17]

Hobsbawm's proclamation of the death of this class struck many as premature since, as he himself admitted, "regions of peasant dominance still represented half the human race at the end of our period."[18] Yet Hobsbawm's views have a respectable pedigree. Marx himself compared peasants to a "sack of potatoes," with little real solidarity and even less class consciousness; he considered them destined for oblivion.

Yet peasants have refused to go gently into that good night to which Collier, Hobsbawm, and Marx have consigned them. Indeed, in 1993, one year before Hobsbawm's book was published, Via Campesina was founded, and over the next decade this federation of peasants and small farmers became an influential presence on the global agriculture and trade scene. The spirit of internationalism, which actively identifies one's class interests with the universal interest of society and was once a prominent feature of the workers' movement, is now on display in the international peasant movement.

Certainly, peasants and rural communities are being marginalized by globalization, and local subsistence production no longer, in many places, provides the escape that it once did for peasants caught up in market relations. Summing up research on "disappearing" peasantries, Deborah Bryceson writes that under conditions of rapid globalization and neglected peasant hinterlands, peasants crossing international borders now provide a massive supply of labor for global capital. Although psychologically many of these peasants still have the notion of a piece of land as a fallback in times of need, "as a class, they face proletarianization by the force of global commodity and labor markets combined with government indifference."[19]

Yet the belief that the land is waiting as a refuge of last resort continues to persist among many peasants turned workers, including those rural migrants in China who are returning en masse to the countryside as factories close amid the spreading global recession.[20] Indeed, peasants show an extraordinary persistence as a class, and perhaps nothing underlines this more than the Mexican peasants who continue to plant corn for subsistence despite being priced out of the market by cheap imports from the United States. In other areas, small farmers have confounded those who have preached their demise by showing that small labor-intensive farms can be far more productive than big ones. To cite just one well-known study, a World Bank report on agriculture in Argentina, Brazil, Chile, Colombia, and Ecuador showed that small farms were three to fourteen times more productive per acre than their larger competitors.[21]

Perhaps the most significant recent development in the long struggle of the peasants as a class has been their organizing internationally to protect their interests from the steamroller of industrial capitalist agriculture. Via Campesina—translated "the peasant way"—has not only been effective in mounting opposition to the World Trade Organization; it has also offered an alternative paradigm for agricultural development, called "food sovereignty." The analysis and appeal of groups like Via Campesina resonate widely because the ability of capital to absorb labor is so limited under the conditions of inequitable globalization that in recent years a significant number of both ex-peasants and semi-proletarians, such as the ex-urban dwellers that have driven the land occupations of the MST (*Movimento dos Trabalhadores Rurais Sem Terra*, or Landless Workers' Movement) in Brazil, have returned to the countryside.

Indeed, not only in the South but also in the North, farmers and others seek to escape the vagaries of capital by reproducing the peasant condition, working with nature from a limited resource base independent of market forces. The emergence of urban agriculture, the creation of networks linking consumers to farmers within a given region, the rise of new militant movements for land—all this, according to analyst Jan Douwe van der Ploeg, indicates a movement of "repeasantization" that has been created by the negative dynamics of "Empire" and that seeks to reverse them. Under the conditions of the deep crisis of globalization, felt widely as a loss of autonomy, "the peasant principle, with its focus on the construction of an autonomous and self governed resource base, clearly specifies the way forward."[22]

Production Paradigms in Conflict

Romanticism, says Collier, is at the root of the increased salience of small-scale agriculture as an alternative to globalized farming in progressive circles. In this he is joined by some intellectuals of the left such as Henry Bernstein, who refers to partisans of the new peasant movements as the "new populists," implying a similarity to the Narodniks of prerevolutionary Russia. But however their conditions and vicissitudes are analyzed by the intellectuals, some of whom even question the label "peasant," small food producers are gathering allies, including many in the governments of the South. These people torpedoed the Doha Round of the World Trade Organization with their stubborn advocacy of "special safeguard mechanisms" (SSMs) against agricultural imports and their designation of key commodities as "special products" (SPs) exempt from tariff liberalization to protect local small-scale farmers. This resistance was incited not only by the significant pressure exerted by groups like Via, but from a growing sentiment in official circles that corporate industrial agriculture could not be allowed to completely restructure the global economy without any accountability except to profitability.

More broadly, as environmental crises multiply, as the social dysfunctions of urban-industrial life pile up, and as industrialized agriculture creates greater food insecurity, the "peasant way" has relevance not only to peasants but to everyone threatened by the catastrophic consequences of global capital's vision for organizing production, community, and life itself. These are the practical realities that lie at the heart of the "romanticization of the peasant" that exercises Collier so much.

Ultimately, the outcome of the battle between the promoters of industrial agriculture and the new peasant movement will be determined by which paradigm of production can better bring about food security—the global market-driven paradigm on the one hand or a local-market–centered paradigm on the other. Bernstein implies, for instance, that only globalized industrial agriculture can meet the huge increase in food demand for which it is largely responsible: "Advocacy of the peasant way largely ignores issues of feeding the world's population, which has grown so greatly almost everywhere in the modern epoch, in significant part because of the revolutions in productivity achieved by the development of capitalism."[23]

Partisans of the peasant way passionately, and justifiably, proclaim that peasants and small farmers continue to be the backbone of global food production, constituting more than a third of the world's population and two-thirds of the world's food producers.[24] Indeed, according to the agroecologist Miguel Altieri,

millions of small farmers in the Global South still produce the majority of staple crops needed to feed the planet's rural and urban populations. In Latin America, about 17 million peasant production units occupying close to 60.5 million hectares, or 34.5% of the total cultivated land with average farm sizes of about 1.8 hectares, produce 51% of the maize, 77% of the beans, and 61% of the potatoes for domestic consumption. Africa has approximately 33 million small farms, representing

80 percent of all farms in the region. Despite the fact that Africa now imports huge amounts of cereals, the majority of African farmers (many of them women) who are smallholders with farms below 2 hectares, produce a significant amount of basic food crops with virtually no or little use of fertilizers and improved seed. In Asia, the majority of more than 200 million rice farmers, few of whom farm more than 2 hectares of rice, make up the bulk of the rice produced by Asian small farmers.[25]

From the perspective of the defenders of peasant agriculture, it is capitalist industrial agriculture, with its wrenching destabilization and transformation of land, nature, and social relations, that is mainly responsible for today's food crises, and it points to a dead end both socially and ecologically. To capital, food, feed, and agrofuels are interchangeable as investment areas, with rates of profit determining where investment will be allocated. Satisfying the real needs of the global majority is a secondary consideration, if indeed it enters the calculation at all. To the critics of capitalist agriculture, it is this devaluation and inversion of real relations into abstract relations of exchange—otherwise known as commodification—that is at the crux of the crisis of the contemporary food system.

The Organization of this Book

The analysis of the food crisis, the spread of capitalist industrial agriculture, and the plight and resistance of the peasantry are the central concerns of this book.

In the first chapter, "Capitalism Versus the Peasant," I will place the current food crisis in the larger panorama of the spread of capitalist industrial agriculture and its displacement of peasant agriculture over the last four hundred years, first in England, then in Europe, then globally. This has been an uneven process marked by advances and stalemates, as it were, though the current period seems to be marked by a particularly aggressive drive of capitalist industrial agriculture to completely displace peasants and small farmers from the process of production in both the North and the South. Following Harriet Friedmann and Philip McMichael, we'll see how this historic process has taken place under different agrifood regimes—various complexes of national and international institutions governing the political economy of international food production. While capitalist industrial agriculture seems to be on the cusp of final victory over peasant and other modes of agricultural production, the current period has also seen widespread recognition of its many social and ecological costs.

The policies of structural adjustment promoted by the World Bank and the International Monetary Fund combined with global trade liberalization under the auspices of the World Trade Organization have been the greatest contributors to the current food crisis. Chapters 2 ("Eroding the Mexican Countryside"), 3 ("Creating a Rice Crisis in the Philippines"), and 4 ("Destroying African Agriculture") detail the swath of destruction that adjustment programs have cut through different regions of the globe.

China has become a global player in agricultural trade, a consequence of developments in the domestic relationship between industry and agriculture, between the countryside and the city. The role of China's peasants, not only in food production but also in the capital accumulation that translated into the country's relatively sudden emergence as the foremost manufacturer in the world is the subject of the fifth chapter, "Peasants, the Party, and Agrarian Crisis in China." The central relationship in China's agrarian order is the tortuous one between the peasantry and the Communist Party, which the peasantry brought to power in the 1940s. In recent years, the party has followed policies, including agricultural trade liberalization, that have led to peasant marginalization and domestic agricultural crisis.

The sixth chapter, "Agrofuels and Food Insecurity," examines how the agrofuel boom has exacerbated the food crisis. Aside from diverting land away from food production, agrofuels have been an engine for the spread of capitalist agrarian relations and the destruction of peasant agriculture. We will also discuss the question of whether agrofuels are, in fact, a viable alternative to fossil fuels in meeting the challenge of climate change.

Beginning with a close look at some key actors in the new peasant movement, the last chapter ("Resistance and the Road to the Future") examines the dynamics of peasant and small farmer resistance to capitalist industrial agriculture, ranging from political protest to international organizing to "peasantization"—the adoption by nonpeasants of peasant or small-scale agricultural practices. These movements underline the fact that contrary to Marx's prediction about its demise, the global peasantry is becoming what he said the working class would become: a "class for itself," or a politically conscious force. These developments, I will argue, represent two things: one, that capitalist industrial agriculture at its moment of seeming triumph has also proved itself to be severely dysfunctional; and second, that small-scale agriculture could be a much more effective response than capitalist agriculture to the social and environmental crises, particularly to global warming. Concluding the chapter will be a critical analysis of the paradigms of "food sovereignty" and "deglobalization" promoted by Via Campesina and other civil society actors as an alternative to the global capitalist regime.

Chapter 1

Capitalism Versus the Peasant

THE FOOD CRISIS, which exploded globally in the form of sharp increases in the prices of basic commodities from 2006 to 2008, has a number of interrelated dimensions. The production and consumption of food has always been socially organized, but the modes of this social organization have varied. Capitalism, or the organization of production to extract surplus value or, broadly, profit, from workers in the production process, has in recent years become more and more dominant as the system that produces the world's food. Peasant production—meaning, in simple terms, the production of food by small farming households, principally for subsistence, but secondarily for monetary gain through the marketing of the surplus product—has for the past few centuries been the main alternative form of production. The current food crisis is, in some ways, a manifestation of what may be the last stage of the displacement of peasant agriculture by capitalist agriculture.

Peasant Elimination and Resistance in Europe

The process of capitalist displacement of peasant agriculture began over four hundred years ago but has never quite been completed. In the seventeenth and eighteenth centuries in England, the wool trade sparked the emergence of a new agrarian elite, drawn from the ranks of the aristocracy and the richer peasant strata, which spearheaded the diffusion of capitalist relations of production in the countryside. Propelling the enclosure movement, when "sheep ate men," as the saying went, were the commercially motivated aristocrat and the large tenant farmer, the two personae of the rural capitalist. The enclosures "had gathered considerable force by about 1760 . . . [and] surged forward at its greatest speed during the Napoleonic Wars, to die out after 1832, by which time [they] had helped to change the English countryside beyond recognition."[1] "Diffusion" is probably the wrong word to describe the commodification of land and labor that resulted in the almost complete elimination of the English peasantry, for it was a process marked by tremendous violence. As Barrington Moore noted:

> Looking back at the enclosure movement as a whole and taking account of the results of modern research, it still seems plain enough that, together with the rise of industry, the enclosures greatly strengthened the larger landlords and broke the back of the English peasantry, eliminating them as a factor from British political life . . . For the "surplus" peasant it made little difference whether the pull from the towns or factories was more important than the push out of his rural world. In either case, he was caught in the end between alternatives that meant degradation and suffering, compared with the traditional life of the village community. That the violence and coercion which produced these results took place over a long space of time, that it took place mainly within a framework of law and order . . . must not blind us to the fact that it was massive violence exercised by the upper classes against the lower.[2]

The expansion of capitalism throughout the world has "constantly reproduced some of the effects that it had in the beginning within its country of origin," the historian Ellen Meiksins Wood has rightly observed.[3] Yet one aspect of the

English experience was rarely repeated: the almost complete displacement of peasant agriculture. Indeed, as Eric Hobsbawm pointedly noted, peasants refused to fade away and remained a "massive part of the occupied population even in industrialized countries well into the twentieth century."[4] In France, capitalist farmers and aristocrats kept the peasants on the soil and used the feudal framework to extract surplus labor from them.[5] One result of these class relations was the creation of the massive peasant discontent that became one of the main drivers of the French Revolution. The salient role of a rebellious peasantry in the Revolution led to the persistence of peasant production, stripped of its exploitative feudal shell, as the base of French agriculture and the institutionalization of peasant influence in national politics. Part of the World Trade Organization's difficulty incorporating global agriculture into a neoliberal framework has been due to obstruction by the French government, under pressure from the powerful French agrarian lobby.

The creation of an international market in grain contributed, ironically, to limiting the spread of capitalist relations of production in Germany and Central Europe. In this zone, which Immanuel Wallerstein characterized as being part of the periphery or semi-periphery of the emerging capitalist world system, commercially oriented agriculture was marked by the hegemony of large landed estates run by traditional magnates relying on repressed peasant labor, with significant areas—what is now southern and western Germany—dominated by smaller peasant holdings.[6]

Settler Agriculture, Colonization, and the First Agrifood Regime

What might be regarded as the surplus peasant labor in Europe created by the spread of agricultural capitalism formed part of the great migration to the Americas and to Australia. In the English settler colonies, transplanted peasants tried to recreate self-reliant subsistence farming on lands from which the indigenous population had been expelled, but lacking Europe's feudal constraints, peasant production or small-scale family farming was more commercialized from the beginning and was not embedded in community or village structures protecting communal traditions of peasant life. White-settler agriculture thus lent itself to greater penetration by capital. Steadily, small scale farmers were displaced by large, capital-intensive farms, though for a long time many farms maintained their family-farm character; that is, they exhibited a familial rather than thoroughly capitalist logic.[7] This commercialized settler agriculture formed part of what Harriet Friedmann and Philip McMichael described as the first international food regime, which emerged in the second half of the nineteenth century.

This regime consisted of two food grids existing under the institutional canopy of a global free-trade system promoted by Great Britain. The first grid, described above, was the settler agriculture that flourished in the vast expanses of the United States, Canada, Australia, and Argentina and which specialized in the production of wheat and livestock that eventually displaced much of European agriculture in providing the wage foods for the industrializing metropolitan economies of Europe. Despite its being part of an international network of capitalist trade, the productive centerpiece of this global system was, as Friedmann and McMichael put it, "commodity production paradoxically based on family labor."[8]

The second grid was the system of colonial production in what is now the South, which specialized in sugar, tobacco, coffee, tea and cocoa for export to expanding European markets as well as raw materials for industry, such as cotton, timber, rubber, indigo, jute, copper, and tin. The distinctive feature of this trade was the "complementarity of colonial exports to metropolitan economies."[9] In much of what is now the global South, the plantation economy specializing in the production of export crops coexisted with a peasant economy growing food crops like rice. One of the classic descriptions of this structure was provided in the case of Indonesia by Clifford Geertz. According to Geertz, a process of "involution" marked agriculture in Java, in which the peasant economy was forced to adopt more and more labor-intensive techniques to keep up production in small rice fields to support a growing population, even as the best lands were appropriated for large Dutch-controlled sugar plantations. Villagers engaged in careful weeding, double cropping, and improved terracing to provide subsistence not only for themselves but also for those among them that provided seasonal labor to the plantations, thus effectively subsidizing the latter.[10] As Geertz put it,

> by keeping their labor force maximally seasonal and their wages low and by preventing Javanese mobility upwards through the ranks of their organization, the plantations encouraged the formation of a very large partial proletariat composed of worker peasants who were neither wholly on the precapitalist side nor wholly on the capitalist side of the dual economy but who moved uneasily back and forth between the two in response to the movement of sugar prices.[11]

In Indonesia, the Philippines and Vietnam as well, the plantations threw back their labor forces' subsistence requirements on impoverished peasants, who struggled to squeeze more and more from less and less land.

This negative symbiosis—from the point of view of the peasant—of the plantation economy and surrounding small farms dedicated to subsistence agriculture was reproduced in Latin America in the form of the notorious "latifundio-minifundio" complex. In parts of Africa, surrounding communities subsisting on land marked by traditional communal tenure performed the role of labor provider and cost absorber that peasants played elsewhere, but with gender playing a key structuring role, for "as men were compelled to work for colonial state projects, women, traditionally the main cultivators, had to work far harder to provide family subsistence."[12]

The Bretton Woods Agrifood Regime

After an interlude of depression, protectionism, and war that saw the end of the first era of globalization, a new food regime emerged that corresponded to the postwar international political economy. The Bretton Woods system was marked by what John Ruggie called "embedded liberalism," that is, an international economic order dominated by national capitalist states that actively traded with and invested in one another while placing market restrictions on these trade and investment relations to ensure that the economic programs, which were based on political and class compromises negotiated in response to the Great Depression, would not be destabilized.[13]

The food regime that corresponded to the Bretton Woods order was one that rested on a system of agricultural and food production in the developed countries that had become capital-intensive and industrialized, mimicking the "Fordist" organization of industry in the postwar era. Though the family farm continued to be a mainstay of the productive system, the sector providing industrial inputs like machines, pesticides, and fertilizer, and the food-processing industry, especially the meat industry, underwent a process of rationalization that was accompanied by a greater centralization and concentration of capital. As Friedmann and McMichael note, "before 1973, the grain companies remained merchant in form, and family grain farms were not directly incorporated into agro-food complexes to nearly the same extent as the specialized production of other agricultural commodities."[14]

In terms of global trade, the Bretton Woods agrifood system was marked by competition among farming interests backed by their respective states. State support took the form of high tariffs and subsidies that mainly benefited the bigger and richer farmers. Resistance to US export dominance led to the protectionist programs that made up the Common Agricultural Policy (CAP), which turned Europe into an agricultural superpower. In fact all the big powers took a protectionist attitude toward agricultural competition; hence the exemption of agriculture from the disciplines of the General Agreement on Tariffs and Trade (GATT).

The Resilient Family Farm

How did small farmers fare in this regime? What was striking was the resilience of the family farm, which continued to be a significant force in US and European agriculture, despite receiving, at best, only marginal benefits from the United States government's subsidies for agriculture: currently, 38 percent of producers who provide 92 percent of US food receive 87 percent of all farm program payments.[15] Why did the family farm persist? Nola Reinhardt and Peggy Barlett find as reasons for survival the limits to the advantages of greater scale in agriculture, the limits to capitalist rationalization posed by the seasonal nature of agricultural production, the biological limits to the advantages of mechanization, the greater capacity of the family farm to react to microclimatic variation and changing biological processes, and a distinct logic that aims not simply at profit maximization but long-term survival as a family enterprise. Unlike the capitalist farm, for instance,

> The farm family, in contrast, is committed to the socialization of children and will accept lower productivity at certain times or in certain enterprises in order to teach children farm skills and the work ethic. In this way, a farm family may sustain, for example, hog production over a low-profit period because it helps to train children. A capitalist farm that must pay workers and managers cannot trade off low returns on profit-seeking goals for high returns on parenting goals.

The distinct calculus of the family farm, they continue, can enable household agricultural production to persist through slow periods that drive capitalist units out of business.

> Family farms can more easily substitute labor for capital during downturns, or increase off-farm employment of family members to tide the household over a difficult period. Alternatively, the household may attempt to maintain farm revenues in a period of declining prices by intensifying the family labor input in order to expand farm output. The calculus of the family farm allows it to cut costs, by accepting a lower marginal return to family labor, more effectively than the capitalist unit, which must continue to meet payrolls or lose skilled labor. This "self-exploitation" of the farm family may not be the principal reason for family farm competitiveness, but it does provide an important survival mechanism that enables technically-competitive household production to survive temporary market downturns.[16]

Developmentalism and Counterinsurgency

In the South, the Bretton Woods regime assumed the form of "developmentalism" or *desarrollismo*, one key feature of which was the advanced capitalist state's tolerance for import substitution policies marked by high tariffs that would allow the development of industries. At the same time, foreign investment was strictly regulated by the newly independent regimes. In East Asia, these tight controls on trade and investment were, in places like Japan, Korea, and Taiwan, the quid pro quo for anti-communist Cold War military alliances with the United States. In agriculture, there was strong protection from imports in the form of outright import bans, quotas, and high tariffs. At the same time export enclaves arose, dependent on special marketing arrangements with specific countries in the North, such as the sugar quota arrangements between the United

States and select developing countries including the Dominican Republic and the Philippines.

Agricultural protection did not, however, translate into a better deal for peasants.

Even as they continued to produce the bulk of foodstuffs in the developing countries, several forces were eroding the position of peasants in the South. One was landlord exploitation. Another was the dissolution of traditional relations of cooperation and mutual dependence by the rapid spread of market relations. "Everywhere," wrote the anthropologist Eric Wolf, "the dance of commodities brought on an ecological crisis. Where in the past the peasant had worked out a stable combination of resources to underwrite a minimal livelihood, the separate and differential mobilization of these resources as objects to be bought and sold endangered that minimal nexus."[17] Landlord exploitation, in fact, often intensified with the spread of the market as landlords became commercial actors seeking to reduce their "social overhead."

A third force destabilizing peasants was the industry-first policies adopted by many countries. The agricultural surplus was commandeered for rapid industrialization through taxes on the peasantry and differential pricing. Here an unlikely alliance emerged that subverted protectionist arrangements in agriculture in the developing countries and translated into peasant distress. The United States used food aid as a way to get rid of its mounting surpluses of grain while buttressing selected allies in the global battle against Communism. As Friedmann and McMichael put it,

> On the import side there was a conjunction of interests between the US, which sought to find new markets for its ever-increasing wheat surpluses, and new states, which sought cheap food to facilitate industrialization . . . Newly independent states, for their part, for their own reasons and with encouragement from international agencies, generally

adopted cheap food policies as part of industrialization programs, and welcomed US wheat when it came as foreign aid. Even when it didn't, the downward pressure on world prices by constant American dumping through aid gave imported wheat a price advantage over domestic grains. Thus proletarianization in the Third World, far from depending on national food markets, occurred through imported American wheat, at the expense of domestic agricultural production. Cheap American grain led to the displacement rather than the commodification of traditional foods.[18]

Not surprisingly, economic marginalization led to discontent and alienation in the countryside. Worried that this could allow peasant-backed radical movements to come to power, as happened in China and Vietnam, US-supported elites made containment of the peasantry one of the objectives of the developmentalist approach.

The prototype of this intervention was provided by the US-supported land reform *cum* rural development in Taiwan and Korea in the 1950s. These measures stabilized the countryside and resulted in a level of peasant prosperity sufficient to act as the stimulus for the first phase of the energetic postwar industrialization in these societies.

The 1960s saw the high-water mark in the US sponsorship of counterrevolutionary agrarian reform, with major efforts launched in Vietnam and Chile. After the failure of these efforts to prevent the left from coming to power in both countries in the early '70s,[19] organizations such as the US Agency for International Development and the World Bank shifted to a strategy of upgrading the "productivity of the poor" via rural development programs in line with the Green Revolution taking place elsewhere in the world. Credit was expanded and technical support was provided to farmers through state agencies funded by the Bank. A key component of this effort to stabilize the countryside and raise rural productivity was subsidies for the purchase of industrially produced seeds, fertilizers, and pesticides. As then World Bank president Robert McNamara told the World Bank Board of Governors in 1974, rural development

> put primary emphasis not on the redistribution of income and wealth—as justified as that may be in our member countries—but rather on increasing the productivity of the poor, thereby providing for a equitable sharing in the benefits of growth.[20]

Rural development would help peasants but not at the expense of alienating the richer sectors in the countryside, as one Bank document frankly explained:

> It may frequently be desirable to design a project so that all sectors of the rural community benefit to some degree. In some countries, avoiding opposition from the powerful and influential sectors of the community is essential if the program is not to be subverted from within. Thus, in some cases where economic and social inequality is initially great, it is normally optimistic to expect that more than 50 percent of the project benefits can be directed toward the target groups; often the percentage will be considerably less.[21]

The aim of the World Bank effort in the countryside was described by one analyst close to the Bank as "defensive modernization," which

> if successful, will create a smallholder sector closely integrated with the national economy. Bank projects will encourage subsistence farmers to become small-scale market producers. With economic ties to other sectors, the farmers will be loath to link their interests to those not yet modernized and will

hesitate to disrupt the national economy for fear of losing their own markets.[22]

On paper, increasing productivity, mitigating poverty, and creating a stable and prosperous *kulak*-style barrier to the forces eroding peasant society might have seemed to be reconcilable objectives. But reality proved unamenable to this vision.

The Neoliberal Utopia and the Countryside

The foreign–aid–backed state-directed effort to stabilize the countryside and increase the productivity of the poor largely failed, and came to an end in the early 1980s. In its place came structural adjustment, a sweeping program of economic liberalization that spread from four experimental countries— Kenya, Turkey, Bolivia, and the Philippines—to cover by the beginning of the 1990s more than 90 developing and transition (postsocialist) economies. Structural adjustment had a number of dimensions and thrusts. It was, for one thing, an ideologically driven enterprise to make economies more efficient, in narrow terms, by liberating market forces from state restraints. In the short term, structural adjustment was a program consisting of radical spending cutbacks and trade liberalization designed to allow governments to accumulate the resources and foreign exchange to pay off their massive foreign debt.

Whether by design or not, structural adjustment set the stage for the intensive subjugation of the countryside to capitalist relations of production by destabilizing the peasant economy, which had been partially sheltered by the containment strategies of the state and the international financial institutions. As Farshad Araghi puts it, "The privatization of the agrarian welfare state created in the national developmentalist era, to the advantage of Northern agribusiness, transnational corporations, and capitalist farms, forms the context in which the relative depeasantization and displacement of the postwar period gave way to the absolute depeasantization and displacement under the postcolonial neoliberal globalism."[23]

The key thrusts of structural adjustment in agriculture were the

> deregulation of land markets and the reversal of land reform policies originating in the national developmentalist era; drastic cuts in farm subsidies and price supports and the disengagement of both postcolonial states and the World Bank from irrigation support; the expanded use of agrarian biotechnologies and the expanded commodification of seeds and seed reproduction; a marked and growing dependence on chemical, biological, and hydrocarbon farm inputs; energy for food crops diverted by an expansion of livestock production for export; expanded cash crop production for export as animal feed; and the export of niche luxury goods, fresh fruits, vegetables, and ornamental flowers for the global centers of overconsumption . . .[24]

Structural adjustment probably wrought greater havoc on peasant agriculture globally than any other force, social or natural.

Global Governance for the Neoliberal Agrifood Order

Structural adjustment imposed by the international financial institutions (IFIs) was one thrust of the emerging paradigm of neoliberal globalization that was in the process of replacing the Bretton Woods system, which was underpinned by Keynesianism. The other thrust was the creation of a system of neoliberal rules that would form the fundamental legal framework for pro-corporate global trade. Agricultural transnationals, along with the pharmaceutical industry and the information industry, were at the cutting edge of this ambitious effort.

Transformations within the US agricultural industry

compelled this outward thrust. Harriet Friedmann identified three pressure points for the creation of a new global food regime. The first had to do with developments in the "wheat complex," which was traditionally the dominant sector of US agriculture in the international arena. Supported by state subsidies, the wheat complex's dumping strategies had provoked a strong challenge from the European Union that led to "anarchy" in world markets that could no longer be addressed by the old Bretton Woods food regime. The second was the "durable food complex," where the sources of change were the loss of complementarity between export agriculture in the South and the food processing industry in the North owing to the substitution of synthetic compounds for tropical products like sugar, and the emergence in the global markets of Southern rivals who specialized in nontraditional exports like cut flowers and soybeans. The third source of pressure for the creation of new governance for the agrifood system was the livestock sector, where complex relations of complementarity and competition emerged, with developing countries entering the drive to provide feedstuffs for livestock in the North or themselves investing in their own domestic livestock industry—with some like Brazil engaging in both enterprises.[25]

According to Friedmann, the wheat, durable food, and livestock complexes were, despite some contradictory tendencies, in the process of becoming integrated, and despite continuing differences at the level of national policies, European and US transnationals were at the cutting edge of the drive to create a highly industrialized agrifood system that was integrated at the global level. "The dominant tendency," she claimed, "is toward *distance* and *durability,* the suppression of particularities of time and place in both agriculture and diets. More rapidly and deeply than before, transnational agrifood capitals disconnect production from consumption and relink them through buying and selling. They have created an integrated productive sector of the world economy, and peoples of the Third World have been incorporated or marginalized—often simultaneously—as consumers and producers."[26]

There was, however, one sector that was especially threatening to peasants and small farmers, because it offered the possibility of wresting almost compete control of the actual physical process of production from them and promised to correct the diseconomies of large-scale production that had allowed the family farm to survive, even in the United States. This was the fast growing genetic engineering (GE) industry. Through the enforcement of intellectual property rights governing its seeds and other organisms and through the development of products such as the so-called "terminator" seeds, which could not be reproduced and saved by the farmer for the next year's crop, GE threatened to complete the circle of peasant dispossession. That biotechnology could in fact provide the death blow to the peasantry that Eric Hobsbawm had prematurely announced is underlined by the geneticist Richard Lewontin:

> By concentrating on the central material link in farm production, the living organism, which at the same time was the most resistant to capitalization, biotechnology has accomplished two steps in the penetration of capital. First, it widened the sphere of input commodity production by including a wide array of organisms that had previously escaped. Second, and more profound, it is making vertical integration possible with the accompanying proletarianization of the farmer. It is this second stage that is the capitalist agriculture of the future.[27]

These were the dynamics within US agriculture in particular that led to the incorporation of agriculture into the World Trade Organization via the Agreement on Agriculture and to the promotion of biotechnology via the Trade-Related Intellectual Property Rights Agreement.

Capitalist Industrial Agriculture:
Triumph or Crisis?

In his analysis of the posture of US agribusiness toward the agricultural negotiations, Philip McMichael claims that the key corporate players favor the use of the WTO to phase out farm programs that subsidize farmers and allow dumping of US grain abroad, arguing that "by reducing price supports, the corporations maximize their ability to structure comparative advantage in the world market, sourcing their inputs from a variety of producing regions incorporated into the 'free' world market."[28] There is some truth to this, and yet the fact of the matter is that the United States has steadfastly refused to significantly reduce, much less dismantle, its farm-support programs, which transfer some $40 billion a year to the agricultural sector from consumers, firms, and taxpayers.[29] Indeed, what seems to be the case is that the key agricultural interests—big farmers, politicians dependent on the farm vote, agro-input suppliers, food processors—have arrived at a modus vivendi that, for the moment at least, severely compromises the United States' free trade stance. This stance combines support for the domestic subsidies with an aggressive drive to open up developed- and developing-country markets to US exports. In other words, free trade for the rest of the world and protectionism for the United States. It was these double standards that torpedoed the Doha Round of the World Trade Organization and prevented the consolidation of the neoliberal system of global governance.

Thus, as the first decade of the twenty-first century comes to a close, an important question confronts us: Is what we are seeing the culmination of the capitalist transformation of agriculture, a process that began four hundred years ago with the capitalist revolution in agrarian relations that preceded the industrial revolution in England? Before the global economic collapse that began in the middle of 2007, agricultural systems throughout the world were being rapidly incorporated into an integrated system in which export-oriented production of meat and grain was dominated by large industrial farms with global supply chains like those run by the Thai multinational Charoen Pokphand (CP) and where technology was continually upgraded by advances in genetic engineering from firms like Monsanto. These trends were accompanied by the elimination of tariff and nontariff barriers, which was facilitating the creation of a global agricultural supermarket of elite and middle-class consumers serviced by grain-trading corporations like Cargill and Archer Daniels Midland and transnational food retailers like the British-owned Tesco and the French-owned Carrefour.

There was little room for the hundreds of millions of rural and urban poor in this integrated global market. They were confined to giant suburban slums, such as the favelas of Brazil, where they had to contend with food prices that were often much higher than the supermarket prices, or to rural reservations, where they were trapped in marginal agricultural activities and were increasingly vulnerable to hunger. Indeed, within the same country, famine in the marginalized sector sometimes coexisted with prosperity in the globalized sector.

This was not simply the erosion of national food self-sufficiency or food security but what some students of agricultural trends call "depeasantization"—the phasing out of a mode of production to make the countryside a more congenial site for intensive capital accumulation.[30] This transformation was a traumatic one for hundreds of millions of people, since peasant production is not simply an economic activity. It is an ancient way of life, a culture, which is one reason displaced or marginalized peasants in India have taken to committing suicide. In the state of Andhra Pradesh, farmer suicides rose from 233 in 1998 to 2,600 in 2002; in Maharashtra, suicides more than tripled, from 1,083 in 1995 to 3,926 in 2005.[31] One estimate is that some 150,000 Indian farmers have taken their lives over the last few years.[32] The global justice activist Vandana Shiva explains why: "Under globalization, the farmer is losing her/his social, cultural, and economic identity as a producer. A farmer is now a 'consumer' of costly seeds and costly chemicals sold by powerful global corporations through powerful landlords and moneylenders locally."[33]

Yet, even as capitalism seemed poised to fully subjugate agriculture, its dysfunctional character was being fully revealed. For it not only condemned millions to marginalization but also severely destabilized the environment in this time of global warming, especially in the form of severe dependency on fossil fuels at all stages of its production process, from the manufacture of fertilizers, to the running of agricultural machinery, to the transportation of its products. It has been estimated that global industrial agriculture employs three calories of fossil fuel energy to produce one calorie of food energy.[34]

Even before the food price crisis and the larger global economic crisis of which it was a part, the legitimacy of capitalist industrial agriculture was indeed eroding and resistance to it was rising, not only from the peasants it was displacing but from consumers, environmentalists, health professionals, and many others who were disconcerted by the mixture of corporate greed, social insensitivity, and reckless science that increasingly marked its advance. Now, with the collapse of the global economy, the integration of production and markets that has sustained the spread of industrial agriculture is going into reverse. "Deglobalization" is in progress "on almost every front," the *Economist* reported, adopting a word I coined nearly a decade ago.[35] The magazine, which has been probably the most vociferous cheerleader of globalization, warned that the globalization depends on the belief of capitalist enterprises

in the efficiency of global supply chains. But like any chain, these are only as strong as their weakest link. A danger point will come if firms decide that this way of organizing production has had its day.[36]

The search for alternatives to the current way of organizing production is, in fact, on, and people are not waiting for capital to provide leadership. As the viability and credibility of global industrial agriculture erode, a sympathetic look is being cast on the peasant and small-scale agriculture that it has sought to displace.

Conclusion

To be fully understood, the global food price crisis of the past few years, which is essentially a crisis of production, must be seen in the context of a centuries-long process of displacement of peasant agriculture by capitalist agriculture. Despite its dominance, capitalist agriculture has never managed to eliminate peasant and family farm-based agriculture, which has survived till now and continues to provide a substantial part of food for national populations, particularly in the South.

The emergence of the international agrifood system since the middle of the nineteenth century has been inflected by this struggle between capitalist agriculture and peasant or family farming. The first international agrifood regime, which emerged in the late nineteenth century under the canopy of free trade provided by the British Empire, consisted of two "grids": in the white-settler colonies, a family farm-based agriculture providing wage foods (cheap foodstuffs consumed by urban workers), mainly wheat and livestock, to the metropolitan economies, and, in the South, capitalist plantation agriculture producing tropical food products for export, with a labor force that was sustained by the surrounding peasant economy.

The succeeding international agrifood regime took shape under the canopy of the postwar Bretton Woods regime. In the North, this rested largely on family-farm based agricultural production, with corporate control of farm inputs, agricultural trade, and the food industry. In the South, peasants and small farmers continued to be the mainstay of food production, with governments seeking to contain and co-opt peasant populations through United States–backed land reform and rural development programs and the maintenance of barriers against cheap imports, though this aim was often subverted by "food aid" programs.

The most recent phase of the development of the global agrifood system has been marked by the effort to establish the World Trade Organization, which would promote the expansion and hegemony of corporate industrial agriculture through the institutionalization of free trade rules and monopolistic intellectual property rights favoring the spread of globally integrated production chains. These chains consist of big input producers, big farms, and big retailers serving a global supermarket of elite and middle-class consumers. This phase has also featured the use of biotechnology, which threatens to completely wrest control of the physical process of production from the farmer and accelerate his or her dispossession and conversion into a rural worker. In its international dimensions, this regime evolved a practice of double standards which sought to impose free trade rules on the South while maintaining huge subsidies for northern farming interests. These double standards severely hampered the legitimacy of the neoliberal project and eventually torpedoed the Doha Round of trade negotiations.

Today, the global economic crisis has derailed the globalist project and inaugurated an era of deglobalization. Industrial agriculture has not only been overtaken by a crisis of legitimacy that has been spreading for some time but the global production and supply chains that it is built on might now wither away. In this context, peasant and small-farmer based agriculture serving local and regional markets might increasingly be seen as a more viable way to organize the production of food.

Chapter 2

Eroding the Mexican Countryside

When tens of thousands of people staged demonstrations in Mexico early in 2007 to protest a sharp increase of over 60 percent in the price of tortillas, many analysts pointed to agrofuels as the culprit. Because of US government subsidies, turning corn into ethanol had become more profitable than growing it for food consumption, and American farmers were devoting more and more of their acreage to corn for ethanol.

The diversion of maize (commonly called corn) from tortillas to biofuel was certainly one of the proximate causes of the skyrocketing prices, though speculation by transnational middlemen on likely trends in biofuel demand may have played a bigger role.[1] However, an intriguing question escaped many observers: How on earth had Mexicans, who live in the land where corn was first domesticated, become dependent on imports of US corn in the first place?

The Mexican food crisis cannot be fully understood without the knowledge that in the years preceding the tortilla crisis, the homeland of corn had been converted to a corn importing economy by free market policies promoted by the International Monetary Fund (IMF), the World Bank, and Washington. The process began with the debt crisis of the early '80s. One of the two biggest developing-country debtors, Mexico was forced to beg for money to service its debt to international commercial banks from the World Bank and the IMF. The quid pro quo for a multibillion-dollar bailout package was what a member of the World Bank executive board described as a program marked by "unprecedented thoroughgoing interventionism" that was designed to pay off the amount advanced by the Bank and the Fund while doing away simultaneously with the high tariffs, state regulations, and government support institutions that the ascendant neoliberal doctrine identified as the barriers to economic efficiency.[2] The program was euphemistically termed "structural adjustment," and agricultural transformation was one of its key components.

Structural Adjustment: The Broader Context

Rolling back the state was the key thrust of structural adjustment, and the Mexican state budget became a central instrument to reduce its role in the economy. As a portion of total government expenditures, interest payments on its debt rose from 19 percent in 1982 to 57 percent in 1988, while capital expenditures dropped from an already low 19.3 percent to 4.4 percent.[3] Since the state was the central driver of the Mexican economy, the consequences were predictable. Mexico's gross domestic product saw no growth between 1982 and 1988, compared with an annual growth of 7 percent in the 1970s. Since the country's population was increasing by about 2.3 percent during this period, this meant that per capita GDP in 1988 had fallen back to its level of the late 1970s.

The slashing of investment by the state—the biggest investor in any economy—was accompanied by, among other things, rapid trade liberalization, and the latter contributed not only to the contractionary spiral but to deindustrialization. As import tariffs were lowered from 50 percent to 20 percent and import licenses were eliminated, bankruptcy cut a huge swath across Mexico's industrial sector. With the closing down of hundreds of factories, the domestic textile and clothing sector shrank radically.[4]

Economic reversal of this magnitude could only have drastic social consequences. Real wage cuts, which amounted to over 41 percent between 1982 and 1988, reduced labor's share of the national income from 43 percent in 1980 to 35 percent in 1987.[5] The number of unemployed rose to 20 percent of the work force and the underemployed to around 40 percent.[6] These conditions drove half the population under the poverty line and worsened an already very unequal distribution of income.[7] The country was trapped in a vicious cycle of sharply decreasing state investment, rapidly contracting demand, and low growth.

Social services were cut viciously. The health budget, for instance, fell from 4.7 percent to 2.7 percent of overall public spending, prompting even the World Bank to acknowledge that the Mexican government "may be underspending on health care."[8] Not surprisingly, infant deaths due to malnutrition were almost triple those in the 1970s.[9]

Despite the absence of genuine economic growth and the bleak social landscape created by structural adjustment, the Mexican government deepened the program into the 1990s, with the coming to power of the neoliberal, technocratic government of Carlos Salinas de Gortari. The privatization program was accelerated with the result that the number of state enterprises was whittled down from 1,155 in 1982 to 285 by 1990.[10] Nine of the eighteen commercial banks taken over by the state during the debt crisis—so that the government could assume their obligations to foreign banks—were returned to private hands.[11] However, these moves produced not the free-market conditions their authors had envisioned but an economy dominated by a select few private interests, where 47 percent of the gross national product was controlled by twenty-five holding companies.[12]

Denationalization was also accelerated. The Salinas government liberalized the restrictive 1973 foreign investment code in 1989, loosening rules for foreign investor participation in areas such as the manufacture of automotive parts and telecommunications services and allowing 100 percent foreign ownership in areas like private education, newspaper publication, and financial services. The privatization and denationalization program was one of the most radical carried out in the developing world, and at the time, the neoliberal government was determined not to let anything get in the way. As Heredia and Purcell wrote:

> The fact that the constitution states that certain key sectors, such as railroads and telecommunications, must be owned by the state was but a minor obstacle. The Senate simply voted to change the constitution, as it has done countless times; indeed, there were over thirty NAFTA [North American Free Trade Agreement] and adjustment-related constitutional amendments during the Salinas administration alone.[13]

The Making of a Financial Maelstrom

A key aspect of the investment liberalization program was capital account liberalization, which came into full force in 1993, when the country became a member of the Organization for Economic Co-operation and Development (OECD), which required members to completely eliminate all restrictions on capital movements. This major development led directly to Mexico's second financial crisis in thirteen years. Much of the incoming foreign investment went to purchase government debt instruments that were denominated in dollars, with speculators, as one account put it, not "paying sufficient attention to the danger that the central bank's currency reserves might not be sufficient to maintain their convertibility into dollars."[14]

The inflow of a huge mass of foreign capital into the country had the effect of creating a real appreciation of the currency, which made Mexico's exports less competitive in world markets. With the dollar inflow triggering a consumption boom among the middle and upper classes, the depressive effects on exports was matched by a rapid rise in the nation's imports, since the deindustrialization that had resulted from structural adjustment ensured that much of the demand for light and durable consumer goods could no longer be met by domestic manufacturing. The upshot was a current account deficit that stood at a whopping 8 to 8.5 percent of gross domestic product by 1994, a development that began to make foreign investors nervous.

Worried about an unstable macroeconomic landscape that they had collectively contributed to, individual investors started pulling out of Mexico in 1994. The yawning current account gap served as another source of instability as currency speculators, local investors, and foreign investors, expecting or betting on a government "correction" of the currency—a devaluation that would reduce the deficit—subjected the peso to a massive assault that subsided only when the government allowed the peso to float, leading it to lose half its nominal value. Financial chaos prompted the United States to hustle up a $50 billion rescue package, most of which went to bail out, in full, the holders of now worthless Mexican government debt instruments.[15] It also brought about pressure from the International Monetary Fund (IMF) to raise interest rates to get foreign investment to flow back in.

The price of this program of capital account liberalization was another round of severe economic contraction, with consequences even worse than those that followed the third world debt crisis in the early '80s: a full-blown depression, with widespread unemployment, the folding up of industries and services, and the shunting of large numbers of people into criminal trafficking in drugs or emigration to the United States. It is hard to deny the claim that both the mass migration northward and the uncontrollable drug trade that has many observers now calling Mexico a "failed state" are linked to the economic and social devastation visited on the country by close to thirty years of structural adjustment and neoliberal reform. It was against this economic and social collapse that the Zapatista movment staged its historic uprising in the state of Chiapas on January 1, 1994, the day the North American Free Trade Agreement (NAFTA) went into effect.

Eroding the Countryside

This depressing picture of the economy lurching from crisis to crisis during two decades of structural adjustment *cum* radical financial liberalization frames the events that unfolded in the Mexican countryside.

Public expenditures for the countryside decreased by half between 1981 and 1986.[16] This translated into a protracted dismantling of the comprehensive state support for agriculture that had been set up in the aftermath of the Mexican Revolution by the Party of the Institutionalized Revolution (PRI) between the 1930s and 1980. The changes were sweeping, as Ana de Ita notes:

> State intervention diminished; credit was individualized; and the rural development bank reduced the amount of credit available for each farmer as well as the number of farmers and crops eligible for credit; subsidies fell; most of the public sector enterprises that manufactured farm inputs, or that collected, marketed, or processed farm products were privatized; state services like agricultural extension, crop insurance and grain storage were privatized; the subsidies that were implicit in floor prices were eliminated, and the subsidies of numerous other public sector goods and services were slashed.[17]

Key agencies were either dismantled or saw their functions reduced. These included the National Seed Producing Company (*Productora Nacional de Semillas*, PRONASE) and the Mexican Fertilizer Company (*Fertilizantes Mexicanos*, FERTIMEX), producers of crucial supplies the neoliberals wanted to turn over to private producers.[18] State provision of irrigation was also radically curtailed. Management and maintenance of irrigation districts was turned over to consumers, with the budget of SARH (the Ministry of Agriculture and Water Resources) decreasing by 74 percent between 1981 and 1987 and by 34 percent between 1991 and 1995.[19]

Contributing to the destabilization of peasant producers were the effects of a program of unilateral liberalization of agricultural trade. This blow to peasant agriculture was followed by an even bigger one in 1994, when the North American Free Trade Agreement went into effect.   Mexico's modest farm trade surplus quickly became a yawning trade deficit, with the latter hitting $2.7 billion by 2003.[20] Today, largely as a result of this fourteen-year-old agreement, Mexico's status as a net food importer sourcing 40 percent of its food in foreign markets has been firmly established.

The corn sector was especially devastated by NAFTA. Although the agreement had a fifteen-year tariff phaseout of protection for corn, US corn flooded in, bringing prices down by half and plunging the sector into chronic crisis. The US corn dump had a number of related causes. One, US government subsidies for corn increased even as Mexican government subsidies were drastically slashed. Two, US export credits to the Mexican government of some $3 billion to buy US corn rose to alleviate the persistent crisis of overproduction in the United States, bringing about what Peter Rosset described as "devastating impacts" on Mexican maize farmers.[21] Third, when the Mexican state marketing agency for corn was shuttered as part of structural adjustment, distribution of both US corn imports and Mexican grain came to be monopolized by a few transnational traders such as the US-owned Cargill and the partly US-owned Maseca operating on both sides of the border. This has given them tremendous power to speculate on trade trends, so that monopoly control of domestic trade has ensured that a rise in international corn prices does not translate into significantly higher prices paid to small producers at the local level.[22] With this monopoly, the companies could magnify real movement in biofuel demand to manipulate the price of corn, as seems to have happened during the tortilla price crisis.

Reversing Land Reform

The broader aim of neoliberal policies was to accelerate the capitalist transformation of the countryside. This went against the system of rural social stabilization practiced by the PRI for decades. Some authors have described the PRI system as social authoritarianism or corporate authoritarianism, in which the peasant population was incorporated into political participation by peasant leaders who were integrated into the party hierarchy. The legitimacy of this system was founded upon the ongoing agrarian reform that occurred throughout the twentieth century, according to Horacio Mackinlay and Gerardo Otero: "That is why the system enjoyed considerable consensus, even if this was a passive consensus in which constituencies lacked their own initiative in political matters. They did what had to be done, knew when to speak up and when to remain silent, whom to communicate with or not."[23]

The key institutional legacy of twentieth-century land reform was the system of *ejidos*, or lands expropriated by the government from landlords for communal use by landless farmers, as well as indigenous agrarian communities that functioned according to the norms of "social property," that is, a collective form of property wherein the beneficiaries' land "could not be sold, rented, or used as guarantee for loans, or be the object of any type of transaction," although the land was given permanently to the beneficiaries and could be transmitted via inheritance from one generation to another.[24]

By the 1990s, continuous land reform had managed to redistribute 103 million hectares, or 56 percent of Mexico's agrarian land and 70 percent of its forests, to 3.5 million *ejidatarios* and communal landholders in 30,322 *ejidos* and communities—

no mean achievement! This meant, among other things, the consolidation of the peasant mode of production, where the priority was production for subsistence, not the market, though what surplus was produced was marketed. This mode of production did not provide for consistent rises in production and productivity, but it did guarantee survival, what Deborah Bryceson has called "subsistence fallback":

> The term "subsistence fallback" refers to the act of producing basic food and non-food for direct consumption and its enabling conditions of production, i.e., access to land and family labor. The existence of the subsistence fallback lends partial autonomy to peasants, provides insurance against risk, and facilitates physical survival. Its value to peasants cannot be overestimated. Even when peasants' command over land or labor is considerably diminished, recourse to their subsistence fallback can give them a negotiating strength and "staying power" that is not fully evident amongst fully landless, proletarianized rural populations.[25]

As market forces exert greater influence in the countryside, Bryceson continues, "the utility of subsistence production for peasants now lies in accommodating to, rather than escaping from, the market. In periods of market decline or strong price fluctuations, subsistence production has an essential cushioning function, safeguarding peasant survival in the face of adversity."[26]

The PRI land reform, while stabilizing the countryside and reducing the appeal of insurgent groups, had the effect of significantly slowing down the commodification of land, thus posing a barrier to the spread of capitalist relations of production in the countryside, so it is not surprising that one the main lines of attack pursued by neoliberals was a reversal of agrarian reform. Neoliberal rhetoric cited the lack of productivity of agriculture and the redundancy of agricultural labor. As Armando Bartra asserts, "Arguing that most small farmers are redundant due to their inability to compete, farm policy in the 1980s explicitly sought to drain off the rural population. A demographic purge was launched to remove some 3 million 'unnecessary' workers from the congested Mexican countryside, freeing agriculture of more than 15 million 'extra' people."[27] Yet, for all its alleged inefficiencies, Mexico was a net food exporter in the late '70s, before structural adjustment, and again in the early '90s, when it posted a modest trade surplus.

Under the guise of ensuring security of tenure, the World Bank drafted an agricultural policy document that sought to eliminate the differences between private property and *ejidal* property and promote the "individualization of the collective functions of the *ejido* and its destruction as a unit of production."[28] Under the slogan of "market-led land reform," the aim of the document and the Mexican government initiatives that were based on it was the alienation of land, its commodification, and its sale, a process that would speed up the spread of full-fledged capitalist relations of production. The famous Article 27 of the Mexican Constitution—which decreed and institutionalized sweeping agrarian reform—was amended, and based on this, there followed a slew of laws aimed at promoting privatization of *ejidal* and communal property and encouraging large-scale investment in agriculture, including foreign direct investment. To implement these measures, the government launched an ambitious nationwide program, the Program for Certification of Rights to Ejido Lands (*Programa de Certificación de Derechos Ejidales y Titulación de Solares*, PROCEDE), which enabled *ejidatarios* to opt for a private property regime, measure individual plots, and eventually obtain certificates for individually owned parcels and for individual parcels of common land.[29]

PROCEDE did not proceed smoothly. It was stymied by, among other things, the peasants' lack of interest in titling their land parcels even as they apparently accepted the program's general objective of privatizing land ownership. In Ana de Ita's view, the lack of interest in titling can be related to cultural and historical criteria, and not only to commercial ones. *Ejidatarios* fought to obtain land, which for them is not merely a commercial resource but rather the space in which their identity is formed and re-created. They are therefore not interested in debilitating the social bonds that integrate the *ejido*, but rather in maintaining and strengthening them.[30]

"Demographic Purge"

Structural adjustment, NAFTA, and the privatization of communal property were ostensibly geared to making agriculture more efficient by lowering the man-to-land ratio and thus increasing productivity. What was neglected by the neoliberal planners was any consideration of where the displaced peasants—some 15 million of them—would go, particularly as Mexico was also undergoing deindustrialization as a result of structural adjustment.

True, promoters of the new agrarian policies said that their aim was to get peasants into the so-called NTAE, or nontraditional agricultural exports, like fruits, vegetables, and cut flowers, for which there was demand in the US market. The problem was that producing these crops was not like producing subsistence crops. There was, first of all, the question of finance. Investment for one hectare of melons ranged from $500 to $700, compared with $210 per hectare of corn. The average investments required for snow peas, broccoli, and cauliflower were even greater, coming to $3,145, $1,096, and $971 per hectare.[31] Financing of this magnitude was simply unavailable to peasants, especially with government credit drying up under structural adjustment. Moreover, producing for export markets followed an industrial capitalist logic quite alien to subsistence production:

There is a constant demand for Mexican winter fruit and vegetable production. Mexican producers have to respond to a fluctuating market, but the flexibility of peasants in producing fresh fruit and vegetables is limited in many ways. Their dependence on foreign capital and the perishability of the produce itself are two major constraints. Land use has to be planned months ahead, based on previous market trends, and *ejido* peasants lack adequate and up-to-date information. The market for perishables is difficult because of seasonal changes in supply, the need for fast and technologically equipped transportation from the packing plant to the market, and hourly changes in prices at the border.

Agricultural and agro-industrial exports are governed by internationally standardized technological requirements. Notwithstanding NAFTA, one of the main problems facing producers is the manipulation by the USA of non-tariff barriers. All Mexican exports to the USA are inspected by the US Department of Agriculture, and must pass through certified packing stations, a procedure which frequently increases costs for farmers.[32]

With the very limited absorptive capacity of industrial agriculture, for many peasants the choice was either the shantytowns of Mexico City or "El Norte," and many opted for the latter. With structural adjustment savaging the economy in the '80s and '90s, migration hit unprecedented levels, with net annual migratory flow in the '90s ten times higher than that recorded for the '80s.[33] By 2006, roughly 10 percent of Mexico's population of about 107 million was living in the United States, estimates show; about 15 percent of Mexico's labor force was working there; and one in every seven Mexican workers was migrating to the United States.[34] There was a strong element of truth in the sardonic comment that, finding eking out a living from agriculture increasingly impossible, Mexico's peasantry simply moved to the United States.

These migrant workers were sending home some $20 billion in remittances, and remittances from family members and relatives explained why, despite their inability to beat the import price, three million farmers continued to grow corn. Remittances, in short, were sustaining peasant production. Perhaps the best explanation for this is provided by Laura Carlsen:

> The remittances have a dual role. First, the money sustains agricultural activities that have been deemed non-viable by the international market but that serve multiple purposes: family consumption, cultural survival, ecological conservation, supplemental income, etc. Second, by sending money home, migrants in the US seek not only to assure a decent standard of living for their Mexican families but also to maintain their *campesino* identity and community belonging that continue to define them in economic exile. Their money, whether individual or organized, subsidizes rural infrastructure, farm equipment, inputs, and labor and conserves cultural identity. The combination of these personal subsidies and subsistence tenacity account for the otherwise unaccountable growth of corn production in Mexico—despite the overwhelming 'comparative advantage' of a distorted international market. They reflect a deep cultural resistance to the dislocation and denial inherent in the free trade model.[35]

Year by year, however, it becomes more and more difficult for these farmers to avoid the fate of many of their fellow corn cultivators and the large numbers of smallholders in sectors such as rice, beef, poultry, and pork who have been forced out of business by subsidized US producers under NAFTA. According to a 2003 Carnegie Endowment report, imports of US agricultural products threw at least 1.3 million farmers out of work. Many, presumably, joined their family members and relatives already in the United States.

Moreover, at some point, this massive emigration of the able-bodied sucks the life out of rural communities. As one account notes, "Entire rural communities are nearly bereft of working-age men. The town of Tendeparacua, in the Mexican state of Michoacán, had 6,000 residents in 1985, and now has 600."[36] Migration also breaks up rural families; ultimately, these communities can offer nothing to draw back the peasants grown used to living in advanced capitalist societies. Looking at the migrant behavior globally, Deborah Bryceson asks whether peasants' negotiating objectives have now "totally reversed":

> During the colonial period, peasants' ultimate escape was posited as local self-sufficient subsistence production; now the ultimate escape, especially in the minds of more youthful peasants, is employment abroad in the North. The global village of neoliberalism has arrived. The IFI [international financial institution] policies of economic liberalization and structural adjustment had held out the promise that the South could become like the North. Many peasants' wanderlust job-seeking is goaded by their impatience or disbelief that this transformation will ever happen in their home areas.

What are the prospects of a change for the better? Not good, and not least among the reasons is the fact that a state controlled by neoliberals continues to systematically dismantle an agricultural support system for peasant producers that was a key legacy of the Mexican Revolution. As Food First's executive director, Eric Holt-Gimenez, sees it, "It will take time and effort to recover smallholder capacity, and there does not appear to be any political will for this—to say nothing of the fact that NAFTA would have to be renegotiated."[37]

Yet one can never dismiss the toughness and resilience of the Mexican peasantry. Especially today, as the neoliberal model collapses, export markets dry up, low-skilled jobs in the United States disappear, and industry spirals into depression owing to the financial crisis, the countryside is likely to see a return of hundreds of thousands of peasant-workers, seeking salvation in the land. Inability of a countryside transformed by agrarian capitalism to absorb these returnees could be a prescription for another agrarian revolution.

Conclusion

The food-price crisis in Mexico must be seen as one element in the concatenation of crises that have rocked that country over the last three decades and brought it to the verge of collapse. The key link between the food crisis, the drug wars, and the massive migration to the North has been structural adjustment.

In the countryside, structural adjustment meant the gutting of the various government programs and institutions that had been built from the 1940s to the 1970s to service the agrarian sector and contain the peasantry. The sharp reduction or elimination of the services they provided had a negative effect on agricultural production and productivity.

The capacity of peasant agriculture was further eroded by the program of unilateral liberalization of agricultural trade in the 1980s and the North American Free Trade Agreement in the mid-1990s, which converted the land that domesticated corn into an importer of the cereal and consolidated the country's status as a net food importer.

The negative effects of structural adjustment and NAFTA-imposed trade liberalization were compounded by the halting of the five-decade-long agrarian reform process as the neoliberals at the helm of the Mexican state sought to reprivatize land, hoping to increase agricultural efficiency by expelling what they felt was an excess agrarian population of 15 million people.

Over twenty-five years after the beginning of structural adjustment in the early '80s, Mexico is in a state of acute food insecurity, permanent economic crisis, political instability, and uncontrolled criminal activity. It may not yet be a "failed state," to use the fashionable term, but it is close to becoming one. It is exhibit A in the case against neoliberalism.

Chapter 3

Creating a Rice Crisis in the Philippines

That the current global food crisis stems mainly from the free-market restructuring of agriculture in the developing world emerges more clearly in the case of rice. Unlike corn, rice is primarily a domestic food crop—less than 10 percent of world rice production is traded. Moreover, there has been no diversion of rice crops from food consumption to agrofuel feedstock. Yet, in the first four months of 2008 alone, prices nearly trebled, from $380 to over $1,000 per tonne. Undoubtedly, the price inflation is due partly to speculation by powerful cartels of wholesalers at a time of tightening supplies. However, as with Mexican corn, the big puzzle is why a number of rice-consuming countries that used to be self-sufficient have come to be severely dependent on imports.

The Philippines provides a grim example of how neoliberal economic restructuring transforms a country from a net food exporter to a net food importer. The country is now the world's biggest importer of rice, regularly sourcing 1 to 2 million tons of its annual rice requirement in the international market. Manila's desperate effort to secure rice supplies at whatever price became front-page news in 2008, and pictures of soldiers providing security for rice distribution in poor communities became emblematic of the global food crisis. Yet this is a country that as late as 1993 was a net food exporter, after achieving a respectable degree of rice self-sufficiency in the late 1970s and the first half of the '80s. What happened to make this country slip into a greater and greater dependency on rice and other agricultural imports?

Containment in the Countryside

The broad contours of the Philippines story are similar to those of Mexico. The dictator Ferdinand Marcos was guilty of many crimes and misdeeds, including failure to follow through on land reform, but one thing he could not be accused of was starving the agricultural sector of government support. To head off peasant discontent and make the peasantry a base of his government, Marcos, much like the PRI in Mexico, launched an agrarian program with three prongs: land reform, building rural infrastructure, and a massive subsidy and lending program to increase agricultural production and productivity.

The Marcos land redistribution program quickly ground to a halt, however, because Marcos feared alienating another group of potential supporters: small and midsize landlords. As a World Bank agricultural officer noted, "Land reform is not amenable to halfway measures. Either the landlord owns the land, or the tiller does. To make that radical change requires more commitment and energy than the Marcos administration has yet been able to demonstrate."[1]

The rural infrastructure program, however, was not unimpressive. The land under irrigation rose from 500,000 hectares in the mid-'60s to 1.3 million in the mid-'80s. And the Masagana 99 (M99) program, consisting of low-interest, no-collateral credit loans tied to the use of high-yielding rice seed varieties, fertilizers, and herbicides, raised rural production and productivity. Patterned after the Puebla Project in Mexico pushed by the PRI, Masagana 99 was viewed as a way of bringing the Green Revolution to smallholders. Part of its appeal lay in the prospect it offered of achieving greater productivity and providing benefits across the board without disturbing entrenched landed interests. A report by a World Bank officer asserted that "one of the most attractive things about M99 was that it could do all this without antagonizing any part of the population [the way] land reform did. With Masagana 99, 'everyone appeared to be a winner.'"[2]

As a program meant to benefit tenants and small farmers, Masagana 99 was a failure. The relatively high outlays it demanded led to large-scale credit defaults among smallholders, and as a World Bank report noted, "a disproportionate amount" of the new technology "has probably gone to landlords, farmers with irrigation, relatively large or progressive farmers, owners of inputs, and creditors."[3] Masagana 99 did succeed, however, in achieving national self-sufficiency in rice production. After years as a chronic rice importer before the '70s and early '80s, the Philippines became not only self-sufficient in rice but also a net exporter. Massive government investment was helping agriculture grow by 5 percent a year. When Marcos fled the country in 1986, it was reported that there were 900,000 metric tons of rice in government warehouses.[4]

Debt Service and Structural Adjustment

In the mid-1980s, growth and development went into reverse as the country entered a period of structural adjustment. The Philippines was one of the guinea pigs, along with Bolivia, Turkey, and Kenya, for the World Bank's new structural adjustment facility for comprehensive economic reform, unveiled in the late '70s. As in Mexico, the aims of structural adjustment included making an economy more "efficient" by exposing it to the winds of international competition, enabling a country to gain the dollars to pay off its foreign debt by pushing it into export-oriented production, and opening up an economy more fully to foreign trade and foreign investment. And as in Mexico, structural adjustment's major impact in the Philippines was to weaken the national economy.

The private sector unraveled in the early 1980s because of trade liberalization coupled with monetary and fiscal tightening at a time of international recession. Describing the fatal conjunction of local adjustment and an international downturn, the late economist Charles Lindsay said, "Whatever the merits of the SAL [structural adjustment loan], its timing was deplorable."[5]

The effective rate of protection for manufacturing provided by tariffs was pushed down from 44 to 20 percent, causing multiple bankruptcies and massive job losses—in short, deindustrialization. The list of industrial casualties included paper products, textiles, ceramics, rubber products, furniture and fixtures, petrochemicals, beverages, wood, shoes, petroleum oils, clothing accessories, and leather goods. The textile industry was practically rendered extinct by the combination of tariff cuts and the abuse of duty-free privileges, shrinking from two hundred firms in 1970 to fewer than ten by the end of the century. As a former finance secretary admitted, "There's an uneven implementation of trade liberalization, which was to our disadvantage." While consumers may have benefited from tariff cuts, he said, liberalization "has killed so many local industries."[6]

The collapse of industry, it must also be noted, took place amid a political crisis that marked the transition from the Marcos dictatorship to the presidency of Corazon Aquino. The downward spiral of private investment was not met by a countercyclical effort by the government to shore up the economy, as would be expected under orthodox macroeconomic management. This was a colossal mistake, and the cause of it was external. International creditors pressured the fledgling democratic government to adopt the so-called "model debtor strategy" in exchange for access to international capital markets. This approach was cast in iron by Aquino's Executive Order 292, which affirmed the "automatic appropriation" from the annual government budget of the full amount needed to service the foreign debt originally instituted by the Marcos government.

The consequences were very much like those in Mexico,

where structural adjustment was gathering speed at roughly the same time. Instead of the government picking up the investment slack, state resources flowed out in debt-service payments. In the critical period 1986 to 1993, an amount coming to some 8 to 10 percent of the Philippines GDP left the country yearly in debt-service payments, adding up to a total of nearly $30 billion[7]—an appalling sum, especially considering that the Philippines' total external debt in 1986 was only $21.5 billion. Furthermore, the onerous repayment terms, subject to variable interest rates, contributed to the practice of incurring new debt to pay off the old, so that instead of showing a reduction, the foreign debt by 1993 had gone up to $29 billion.[8]

Interest payments as a percentage of total government expenditure went from 7 percent in 1980 to 28 percent in 1994. Capital expenditures, on the other hand, plunged from 26 to 16 percent. Debt servicing, in short, became, alongside wages and salaries, the number one priority of the national budget, with capital expenditures being starved of outlays.[9] Since government is the biggest investor in the Philippines—indeed, in any country—the radical stripping away of capital expenditures goes a long way toward explaining the stagnant 1 percent average yearly GDP growth rate in the 1980s and the 2.3 percent rate in the first half of the 1990s.[10]

The antigrowth implications of the state's being deprived of resources for investment were very clear to Filipino economists during the mid-'80s. In 1985, professors at the University of the Philippines authored the so-called White Paper, warning: "The search for a recovery program that is consistent with a debt repayment schedule determined by our creditors is a futile one and should therefore be abandoned."[11]

The outflow of government resources and the shrinking of capital expenditures continued into the first years of the new millennium. In 2005, according to the World Bank, 29 percent of government expenditures[12] went to interest payments to both foreign and domestic creditors and 12 percent to capital expenditures. This configuration of government spending prompted the UP School of Economics faculty to complain once again that the budget left "little room for infrastructure spending and other development needs," though they did not follow through on the policy consequences of their analysis.[13] In their criticism they were joined, cruelly, by the debt-service-first enforcers themselves, the World Bank. In a classic example of blaming the victim, the Bank wrote in a 2007 policy brief:

> The Global Competitiveness Index ranks the Philippines at only 71 out of 131 countries, rating the country particularly poorly on a majority of the infrastructure indicators. The quality of transport infrastructure (which includes roads, railways, ports, airports, and logistics) is a particularly serious concern, with consequences for trade-related transaction costs and overall competitiveness. Recent assessments indicate that transport infrastructure is poorly maintained and badly managed, with years of underinvestment, especially in maintenance.[14]

It is not surprising that with low government capital expenditures, total fixed investment has remained anemic, running at only 14 percent of GDP, which the World Bank noted is "substantially lower even than during the deep recession in the first half of the 1980s and substantially lower than in most other larger East Asian economies."[15] Durable equipment investment, it added, reached a historic low in 2007.[16]

Agriculture under Adjustment

Among the items cut most sharply was spending on agriculture, which fell by more than half, from 7.5 percent of total government spending in 1982 under Marcos to 3.3 percent in 1988 under Aquino.[17] Coupled with an international recession, the depressive impact of structural adjustment in the countryside was so great that migration from the lowlands escalated, flowing not only to the cities but to the uplands, putting great pressure on the fragile ecology of that area.[18] The World Bank and its local acolytes were not worried, however, since part of the purpose of the whole belt-tightening exercise was to get the market and the private sector to march into the breach and energize the countryside. But the country's agricultural capacity quickly eroded. The amount of cultivated land covered by irrigation stagnated at 1.3 million out of 4.7 million hectares. By the end of the '90s, only 17 percent of the Philippines' road network was paved, compared with 82 percent in Thailand and 75 percent in Malaysia. Crop yields sagged across the board, with the average of 2.8 metric tons of rice per hectare way below yields in China and Vietnam,[19] where interventionist governments took an active role in promoting rural production. Already weak and riddled with loopholes, the post-Marcos agrarian reform program shriveled, deprived of funding for support services that had been the key to successful land reforms in Taiwan and Korea.

What this discouraging panorama underlines is that as in Mexico, peasants in the Philippines were confronted with the retreat of the state from the role of comprehensive provider—support that peasant farmers had come to depend on.

Free Trade's Assault on Agriculture

The cutbacks in agricultural programs imposed by the IMF and World Bank were followed by trade liberalization, and the Philippines' entry into the World Trade Organization (WTO) in 1995 had the same effect that adherence to NAFTA had in Mexico.

Membership in the WTO and its Agreement on Agriculture required the Philippines to eliminate quotas on all agricultural imports and permit a certain amount of each commodity to enter at low tariff rates. The country was allowed to maintain a quota on rice imports, but it was nevertheless required to admit the equivalent of 1 percent of domestic consumption in 1995, rising to 4 percent in 2004. In any event, because rice production had been starved of state support and was gravely weakened, the government ended up importing more than it was obligated to in order to supply local needs. These imports, which rose from 263,000 metric tons in 1995 to 2.1 million metric tons in 1998, had the effect of depressing the price of rice, discouraging farmers and exacerbating the country's fall behind the production rate of its two top suppliers, Thailand and Vietnam.[20]

The WTO requirements didn't just destabilize rice production, they barreled through the rest of Philippines agriculture like a super-typhoon. Corn farmers in Mindanao, reported the trade analyst Aileen Kwa, "have been wiped out. It is not an uncommon sight to see farmers there leaving their corn to rot in the fields as the domestic corn prices have dropped to levels [at which] they have not been able to compete."[21] Swamped by cheap corn imports, a large part of it subsidized American grain, farmers sharply reduced the land devoted to corn, from 3,149,300 hectares in 1993 to 2,510,300 hectares in 2000.[22] The travails of corn were paralleled in other sectors: massive importation of chicken parts nearly killed the chicken parts industry, while surges in imports destabilized the poultry, hog, and vegetable industries.[23]

During the campaign to ratify WTO membership in 1994, Philippine government economists, coached by their World Bank handlers, promised that the losses in corn and other traditional crops would be more than compensated for by the emergence of a new export industry specializing in the production of so-called "high-value-added" crops such as cut flowers, asparagus, broccoli, and snow peas. This industry did not materialize. Neither did the 500,000 new agricultural jobs that were supposed to be created yearly by the "magic" of the market; instead, employment in agriculture dropped from 11.2 million people in 1994 to 10.8 million in 2001.[24]

The magic didn't work. All that came from the one-two punch of IMF-imposed adjustment and WTO-imposed trade liberalization was the swift transformation of an agricultural economy with a high degree of self-sufficiency into one that was permanently import-dependent, its small farmers steadily marginalized. It was a wrenching process, the pain of which was captured by a government negotiator during one of the sessions of the WTO's Agricultural Committee in Geneva. "Our agricultural sectors that are strategic to food and livelihood security and rural employment," he told the body, "have already been destabilized as our small producers are being slaughtered by the gross unfairness of the international trading environment. Even as I speak, our small producers are being slaughtered in our own markets, [and] even the more resilient and efficient are in distress."[25]

The Agreement on Agriculture opened the floodgates to subsidized foreign foodstuffs while reduced tariffs deprived the government of revenue for capital expenditures, including for agriculture. In short, the hemorrhage of payments on the foreign debt blew a hole on the expenditure side, and trade liberalization blew a hole in state income. The trade liberalization that started with Executive Order 264—which phased in, beginning in 1994, a radical program to unilaterally reduce all tariffs to 0 to 5 percent by 2004—resulted in radically decreased customs collections in a very short period of time. In the period 1995 to 2003, while the value of imports grew by 40 percent, customs collections of import duties declined by 35 percent; imports rose from US $25.5 billion in 1995 to $37.4 billion in 2003, but import duties fell from PHP64.4 billion to PHP41.4 billion.[26] As a percentage of GDP, total customs collections fell from 5.6 percent of GDP in 1993 to 2.8 percent in 2002. As a percentage of government revenues, customs duties and taxes from international trade fell from 29 percent in 1995 to 19 percent in 2000 at a time when hardly any new revenue sources were being made available.[27]

Combined with the outflow of debt-service payments, the collapse in customs revenues precipitated a fiscal implosion, which made it even more difficult for government to finance the capital expenditures that were necessary to "crowd in" both domestic and foreign investment in order to decisively lift the country from the stagnation of the '80s and '90s. A former finance chief could not but admit the obvious—that it was not so much failure to increase taxation but the drive to decrease import taxation that mainly accounted for the crisis in government revenue: "The severe deterioration of fiscal performance from the mid-1990s could be attributed to aggressive tariff reduction."[28]

Agrarian Reform and Counterreform

The Philippines did not experience the agrarian counterreform that took place in Mexico beginning in the early 1980s. The continuing volatility in the countryside, which was marked by a communist insurgency, precluded this option. Thus, following the stalled Marcos land reform, pro–land reform forces mobilized under the Aquino administration for a more all-encompassing program. They were disappointed, however, when a strong landlord opposition in the Congress managed to water down the Comprehensive Agrarian Reform Program (CARP) legislation passed in 1988. Republic Act 6657 allowed landlords to retain five hectares of their property, plus three hectares for each legitimate heir.

Implementation of the law required a protracted battle from which the landlords eventually emerged victorious. A key turning point occurred early on when President Aquino and her family refused to allow their huge estate Hacienda Luisita to be subject to redistribution to tenant farmers and workers. Hesitant (and self-interested) administrations like Aquino's and those of the presidents who succeeded her were no match for determined resistance from landlords. To avoid redistribution

they subdivided their land among family members, sold the
land to dummies or proxies, converted land to commercial and
industrial uses to take advantage of the loopholes in the law,
tied up the process in the courts, cut off funding for reform,
and engaged in outright physical resistance. Certificates of
land ownership (CLOAs) were routinely challenged and
beneficiaries were kept hanging as landlords remade the facts
on the ground. In a number of cases, peasants who had received
CLOAs were ordered off by the authorities, even if they had
already taken possession of the land and had been working it
for years.[29] Intimidation and assassination of activists, including
land-reform advocates such as Rene Penas and Eric Cabanit,
who were leaders of influential peasant organizations, became
commonplace during the presidency of Gloria Macapagal-
Arroyo.

Cutting off funding for reform was a critical weapon, and
during the Arroyo administration, the budget for land acquisition
was repeatedly slashed by Congress, with little effort by Arroyo,
herself a landlord like President Aquino, to restore the level
of funding that was needed to make redistribution successful.
As one study, cosponsored by the Department of Agrarian
Reform and the German aid agency GTZ (German Technical
Cooperation), noted, "From a financial perspective, the glaring
lesson learned is that the program has not been a priority of all
branches of government. Even if the Executive Branch could
harness public interest to promote development interventions
such as CARP, a landlord-dominated Congress could choke
off the program by not providing the necessary support for its
logistical requirements."[30]

It must be noted that in the land reform process, the World
Bank was on the side of the landlords, calling for a deemphasis on
redistribution and proclaiming that "CARP must not undermine
the functioning of land markets as they are the most effective
way to redistribute agricultural land from less to more efficient
producers."[31] Part of the Bank's wariness stemmed from the fact

that a substantial number of agrarian reform beneficiaries were rice farmers, and the Bank considered rice farming inefficient.[32] But the strategic aim of the Bank was more important, and this was to eventually replace the peasantry with more capitalist-oriented landholders as the base of agricultural production via an approach called "market-led agrarian reform" (MLAR).

Essentially, MLAR was the latest phase in the transformation of agriculture from precapitalist or feudal relations of production to full-fledged market relations. As three eminent students of land reform put it, "MLAR is integrally and intimately intertwined with expanded commodification, in that within the context of neoliberal agrarian restructuring MLAR seeks to deepen land markets and hence the status of land as an alienable commodity."[33] There are winners and losers in MLAR. The winners are the landlords and rich peasants who are most effective at reducing the unit cost of production and thus are more profitable. The losers are the peasants who cannot adapt from predominantly family-oriented production to predominantly market-oriented production and thus lack the resources to be competitive. Despite the rhetoric of reform, the egalitarian thrust and social justice dimension were relegated to the background of market-led agrarian reform. Landlords weren't compelled to give up their land, and so they were happy with MLAR.

In 2008, twenty years after it began, the land-reform program had transferred only 17 percent of the 1.5 million hectares or private land that CARP had slated for redistribution.[34] This was hardly encouraging. But equally important, the tremendous uncertainties, confusion, and conflicts triggered by the process thwarted production and productivity. Land reform and productivity increases in Taiwan, Korea, and Japan succeeded only because the reform measures had solid backing from the government, gave definitive legal ownership to tenant farmers, had more than adequate financing, and provided effective support services. The land-reform process in the Philippines has had none of this, and it shows in the outcome. As the land-reform expert James Putzel noted:

> Back in 1961, the Philippines was about six times more
> productive, in terms of productivity per laborer employed
> in agriculture, than the regional average. However, already
> the country had fallen behind South Korea, still a very
> poor economy, but with three times the productivity
> of the Philippines, in no small part due to the rapid land
> redistribution that occurred there after the Korean War.
> Today, the Philippines labor productivity in agriculture is
> only twice the regional average and only one tenth of that
> achieved in South Korea. Land redistribution alone cannot
> make up the gap, but it must remain an important part of
> any plan dedicated to putting this struggling middle-cone
> country, ridden by persistent conflict and developmental
> performance, into the ranks of Asian developers.[35]

In June 2009, the agrarian reform was extended for five
years, with Congress appointing some 100 billion pesos for the
compulsory acquisition of land. It remains to be seen, however,
if this extension would jumpstart the process from its state of
stagnation.

But the fate of agrarian reform in the Philippines must also be
seen in the light of what had become agriculture's increasingly
marginal role in the development strategy of the country.
Neglect, structural adjustment, trade liberalization—all this had,
over the years, severely weakened Philippines agriculture. Far
from seeking ways to reverse the crisis in the countryside, the
administration of Gloria Macapagal-Arroyo did not see any hope
in agriculture, even though close to 50 percent of the work
force continued to be dependent on it. For the administration,
the future lay in the export of labor, attracting more outsourced
services from US firms, and mining. Insofar as agriculture was
seen as having a role to play, it was in making land available
to Chinese, Qatari, and other foreign enterprises that would

produce food crops, or more recently agrofuel feedstock for exclusive export to their land-poor homelands. For a country where seven out of ten rural inhabitants were landless, this was sure to spell big trouble.

Conclusion

Like Mexico in the case of corn, the Philippines made headlines early in 2008 for its massive deficit in rice.

From a net food exporter, the country had become a net food importer beginning in the mid-1990s, and the essential reason was the same as in Mexico—that is, the subjugation of the country to a structural adjustment program that was one of the first in the developing world. The program involved a massive reduction of funding for rural programs that were set up during the Marcos dictatorship in the latter's effort to convert the peasantry into a pillar of the regime.

The deleterious effects of structural adjustment, which sought to channel the country's financial resources to the payment of the foreign debt, were compounded by the entry of the country into the World Trade Organization in the mid-1990s, which required it to end the quotas on all agricultural imports, except for rice. In one commodity after another, Filipino producers were displaced by imports.

Contributing to the decline of agricultural productivity was the stuttering halt of the agrarian reform program, successfully stymied by landlords and its own lack of effective support services such as those that accompanied the successful land reform processes in Taiwan and Korea.

Today, the status of the Philippines as a permanent importer of rice and, more generally, a net food importer is implicitly accepted by a government that does not view the countryside as an essential element in the nation's economic development, except perhaps as sites for plantations rented out to foreign interests.

Chapter 4

Destroying African Agriculture

African agriculture is a case study of how doctrinaire economics can destroy a whole continent's productive base. At the time of decolonization in the '60s, Africa was not just self-sufficient in food but was actually a net food exporter, averaging 1.3 million tons in food exports a year between 1966 and 1970.[1] Today, the continent imports 25 percent of its food, with almost every country being a net food importer.[2] Hunger and famine have become recurrent phenomena, with the last few years alone seeing food emergencies break out in the Horn of Africa, the Sahel, Southern Africa, and Central Africa.[3]

During the recent food price crisis, Africa saw its net food imports increase to 1.6 percent of gross domestic product (GDP) in 2007. "All else being equal," the United Nations reported in *World Economic Situation and Prospects*, "the incidence of extreme poverty in sub-Saharan Africa may have risen by almost 8 percentage points, implying that the recent food price increases have more than offset the poverty reduction achieved between 1990 and 2004."[4]

African agriculture is in deep crisis, and the causes are many, including civil wars and the spread of HIV/AIDS. However, a very important part of the explanation is the phasing out of government controls and support mechanisms under the structural adjustment programs to which most African countries were subjected in exchange for IMF and World Bank assistance to service their external debt.

Before Structural Adjustment

As in Mexico and the Philippines, structural adjustment was preceded by heavy state involvement in agricultural production in the 1960s and 1970s as the newly independent governments saw agricultural growth as the fast track to economic development. Peasant agriculture became the key growth sector for a complex of reasons, as Deborah Bryceson notes:

> What large-scale trade and industry existed at the time of independence was usually in the hands of non-Africans. African policy-makers, keen to effect Africanization of the economy as rapidly as possible, concentrated on the sector that was overwhelmingly African. Having played a pivotal role in the achievement of political independence, newly formed African governments were highly responsive to their peasant constituencies. Peasants' sensitivities were incorporated in tax reform: hut and poll taxes, so deeply associated with colonial overlordship, were largely abolished. Welfare issues came to the fore: food security became a *sine qua non* of post-colonial government policy and emphasis was placed on investments in rural water supply, health, and educational facilities.[5]

The close support of state elites for agriculture led to the establishment of marketing boards and parastatals (government-affiliated firms) in the 1970s. Export agriculture was developed and agricultural production grew, but this involved greater and greater subsidies for fertilizers and other inputs. Subsidization came from deficit financing and overvaluation of currencies to keep import prices of agricultural inputs low. Support also came in the form of rural development projects such as export-crop promotion, food-crop support, fertilizer support, and input programs financed by the World Bank and other development agencies. Though these were run by state or parastatal agencies, notes one expert, "their shape and size was every bit as much decided by donors and their consultants, who usually designed the programs and always had the final say on funding."[6]

Subsidization was, however, just one face of the government's relationship with the peasants. Hand in hand with subsidies came the extraction of the peasants' surplus through taxes or the underpricing of rural produce. As was the case in many other places in the postwar period, industrialization was seen as a main route to development, and it "was a corollary of this that industrial investment would involve a certain amount of value extraction from the existing foundation of national production, namely the peasantry."[7] The peasant surplus eventually came to support not just industrialization but also the expanding populations of the cities.

Nevertheless, there were important advances in agriculture. Maize yields burgeoned with the help of better inputs and fertilizers subsidized and distributed by several African governments.[8] Overall, as one recent study notes, sub-Saharan Africa experienced "quite robust growth between 1970 and 1973, when its per capita income grew at an annual average of nearly 3 percent."[9]

The Berg Report

This phase of agricultural modernization came to an end in the late '70s. The conjunction of a financially overstretched state, severe indebtedness to multilateral agencies, two massive oil price hikes, and the ascendancy of neoliberal thinking in Washington, DC, brought this phase of agrarian history—the era of "agricultural modernization"—to a close in the early 1980s. The new thinking descended on Africa with a vengeance in a World Bank document titled *Accelerated Development in Sub-Saharan Africa,* also known as the Berg report, after its coordinator Elliot Berg. The report "set out a tough critique of African governments for failing to provide incentives for agricultural growth, discouraging the private sector, poor public sector management and investment, and poor exchange rate and trade policies."[10]

The Berg report represented a 180-degree turn for the Bank, which had been one the biggest financiers of the state-led agricultural modernization program in the '70s. But there was little recognition in the Berg report of the Bank's key role in the state-led approach and there was little appreciation of the shocks created by the oil price hikes, which simply threw countries' external accounts off balance. Instead, the economic crisis was placed squarely on the development policies followed by African governments. "Never before had the Bank been as publicly critical of such a large group of funders," noted one report.[11]

The timing was critical, since with the onset of the debt crisis, so many governments had no one to turn to as they sought to service their debts other than the World Bank and the IMF. Not surprisingly, shortly after the report was issued, governments started to follow their recommendation to "adjust." During the first phase, which took up most of the 1980s, the focus was on devaluation, cuts in government spending, and tighter control over parastatals. The second phase prioritized privatization or the closure of public agencies and encouraged an "enabling environment" for private enterprise.[12]

But instead of triggering a new era of growth and prosperity led by the private sector and the market, structural adjustment accelerated Africa's downward spiral.

Why Adjustment Failed

Why did structural adjustment in Africa fail so miserably, a contention that is no longer disputed by the World Bank? One can explain it using a fairly simple model based on commonsense economics that I outlined in an earlier work:[13]

- Typically, SAPs [structural adjustment programs] begin with stabilization measures such as tightening the money supply, letting interest rates rise, reducing government spending, and cutting wages. Inevitably, this forces a contraction of the economy.
- When devaluation is added to this policy of monetary and fiscal austerity to promote exports and earn foreign exchange, it escalates the contractionary effects by raising the local cost of imported capital and intermediate goods, leading to the " 'policy overkill' for which the IMF is (un) justly famous."[14]
- Economic contraction discourages private investors, and left to itself, the market does not automatically produce the signals that would renew private-investor confidence in a declining economy.
- Nor does liberalization necessarily spark investment and growth in the agricultural sector, since the simplistic focus on lifting price controls on commodities fails to address the deeper structural, infrastructural, and technological barriers to production that are usually addressed by state-supported programs—which are, however, in the process of being dismantled in the name of fiscal discipline.
- Where liberalization does lead to a rise in production, rising export income can trigger higher investment. But after an initial rise as producers respond to the SAP's export incentives, export income falls as world prices of the country's export commodities fall, precisely in response to the rising supply of the commodities stimulated by SAP programs in countries specializing in the same commodities. Besides, the lion's share of any income gain is now being allocated not to investment, but to debt servicing.
- This leaves "public capital formation [as] the only vehicle for stimulating investment after adverse shocks."[15] But with its expenditures being shut down in order to reduce

its role in economic life, the state cannot step in to reverse the decline in private investment.

- The end result of such macroeconomic management is that the economy becomes stuck in a low-level trap, in which low investment, increased unemployment, reduced social spending, reduced consumption, and low output interact to create a vicious circle of stagnation and decline, rather than a virtuous circle of growth, rising employment, and rising investment, as originally envisaged by World Bank theory.

Structural adjustment was supposed to correct the urban–industrial bias of the period of protectionist import substitution prior to the 1980s. Instead, it devastated industry and crippled agriculture. In Ghana, which was one of the few "successful" examples of structural adjustment that the World Bank loved to cite, adjustment was nothing short of a calamity for industry. Large sections of industry, especially the most modern sectors, were destroyed by the import competition triggered by trade, with survivors and new entrants into industry being mainly "very small-enterprise making low-income or localized products."[16] Employment in manufacturing fell from a peak of 78,700 to 28,000 in just six years, from 1987 to 1993.[17]

The experience was paralleled elsewhere: the ten industries in Africa that were the fastest-growing employers in the 1970s were the fastest growing disemployers in the 1980s.[18] The technological knowledge that had been accumulated in the first two decades of African industrialization was "dissipated by shock therapy that [led] to massive industrialization."[19] So bleak was the resulting landscape that two Africa specialists warned that the long-term result of structural adjustment "could well be to foreclose the possibility of significant industrialization" on the continent.[20]

Adjusting Agriculture

The situation in agriculture was similar. Lifting price controls on fertilizers while simultaneously cutting back on agricultural credit systems simply led to reduced applications, lower yields, and lower investment. One would have expected the non-economist to predict this outcome, which was screened out by the Bank and Fund's free-market paradigm. Moreover, reality refused to conform to the doctrinal expectation that the withdrawal of the state would pave the way for the market and private sector to dynamize agriculture. Instead, the private sector saw reduced state expenditures as creating more risk and failed to step into the breach. In country after country, the opposite of neoliberal predictions occurred: the departure of the state "crowded out" rather than "crowded in" private investment.[21] In those instances where private traders did come in to replace the state, an Oxfam report noted, "they have sometimes done so on highly unfavorable terms for poor farmers," leaving "farmers more food insecure, and governments reliant on unpredictable aid flows."[22] The usually pro-private-sector *Economist* agreed, admitting that "many of the private firms brought in to replace state researchers turned out to be rent-seeking monopolists."[23]

What little support the government was allowed to muster was channeled by the Bank into export agriculture to generate the foreign exchange earnings the state needed to service its debt to the Bank and the Fund. But, as had happened in Ethiopia in the lead-up to the famine of the early 1980s, good land was dedicated to export crops, with food crops forced into more and more unsuitable soil. Moreover, because the Bank encouraged several economies to focus on export production of the same crops, overproduction triggered price collapses in international markets. For instance, the very success of Ghana's program to expand cocoa production triggered a 48 percent drop in the international price of cocoa between 1986 and 1989, threatening, as one account put it, "to increase the vulnerability of the entire

[Ghanaian] economy to the vagaries of the cocoa market."[24] In 2002 to 2003, a collapse in coffee prices contributed to another food emergency in Ethiopia.[25]

As in many other developing countries, structural adjustment in Africa was not simply underinvestment but state divestment. But there was one major difference. In Latin America and Asia, the Bank and Fund confined themselves for the most part to macromanagement, or supervising the dismantling of the state's economic role from above, leaving the dirty details of implementation to the bureaucracy. In Africa, where they dealt with much weaker governments, the Bank and Fund micromanaged, reaching down to make decisions on how fast subsidies should be phased out, how many civil servants had to be fired, or even, as in the case of Malawi, how much of the country's grain reserve should be sold and to whom.[26] In other words, Bank and IMF resident proconsuls reached to the very innards of the state's involvement in the agricultural economy to rip it up.

One upshot of this drastic forced withdrawal of the state from agricultural production, according to Kjell Havnevik and his associates, was that "the blooming of a potential green revolution fostered by policies of several African states during the 1970s was nipped in the bud. Unlike the green revolution of India, Indonesia, and the Philippines, which had afforded farmers several years of state-supported subsidy, Africa's green revolution was stillborn."[27]

Global Trade and Local Ruin

Compounding the negative impact of adjustment were unfair trade practices on the part of the EU and the United States. Trade liberalization allowed low-priced subsidized EU beef to enter and drive many West African and South African cattle raisers to ruin. The same dynamics operated when it came to cereals. Africa's share of world cereal imports rose from 8 percent in 1975 to 16 percent by 1998. In the case of rice, imports went from 11 percent in 1971 to 28 percent in 1991 and 23 percent in 1997.[28] Two key causes, cited by the Africa experts Christopher Stevens and Jane Kennan, were "the easy availability of food aid [that] . . . depressed agricultural production" and "artificially low world prices, resulting from subsidies paid by Northern governments to their farmers."[29]

Western dumping drastically limited options for farmers. For instance, wheat imports skyrocketed in West Africa, with imports to Burkina Faso going up by 84 percent between 1996 and 2000. When their wheat production was rendered noncompetitive by these subsidized imports, farmers in French-speaking West Africa invested heavily in cotton as an alternative to food production, calculating that their costs of production made them very competitive vis-à-vis other cotton producers. But their advantage did not last long.[30] Benefiting from subsidies legitimized by the WTO's Agreement on Agriculture, US cotton growers offloaded their cotton on world markets at between 20 to 55 percent of the cost of production, bankrupting in the process the West African and Central African cotton farmers.[31] West African farmers ended up losing $200 million a year between 1997 and 2001.[32]

These dismal outcomes were not accidental. As then US agriculture secretary John Block put it at the start of the Uruguay Round of trade negotiations in 1986, "the idea that developing countries should feed themselves is an anachronism from a bygone era. They could better ensure their food security by relying on US agricultural products, which are available, in most cases at lower cost."[33] What Block did not say was that the lower cost of US products stemmed from subsidies, and these became more massive with each passing year, even though the WTO was supposed to phase out all forms of subsidy. From $367 billion in 1995, the first year of the WTO, the total amount of agricultural subsidies provided by developed country governments rose to $388 billion in 2004.[34] Subsidies now account for 40 percent of the value of agricultural production in the European Union and 25 percent in the United States.[35]

The social consequences of structural adjustment *cum* agricultural dumping were predictable. According to Oxfam, the number of people living on less than a dollar a day more than doubled to 313 million people between 1981 and 2001—or 46 percent of the whole continent.[36] The role of structural adjustment in creating poverty, as well as severely weakening the continent's agricultural base and consolidating import dependency, was hard to deny. As the World Bank's chief economist for Africa admitted, "We did not think that the human costs of these programs could be so great, and the economic gains would be so slow in coming."[37]

That was, however, a rare moment of candor. As the Oxford University political economist Ngaire Woods pointed out, the "seeming blindness of the Fund and Bank to the failure of their approach to sub-Saharan Africa persisted even as the studies of the IMF and the World Bank themselves failed to elicit positive investment effects."[38]

Malawi: From Compliance to Defiance

Stubbornness led to tragedy in Malawi.

It was a tragedy preceded by success. For several years, the government had supplied "starter packs" of free fertilizers and seeds to the poorest Malawian families. The experiment was so successful that in 1998 and 1999, the government expanded the program to include small landholders.[39] The result was a national surplus of corn. What came after will definitely have to be enshrined as a classic case study in a future book on the ten greatest blunders of neoliberal economics.

The World Bank and other aid donors forced the drastic scaling down and eventual scrapping of the program, arguing that the subsidy distorted trade.[40] Without the free packs, food output plummeted. In the meantime, the IMF insisted that the government sell off a large portion of its strategic grain reserves to enable the country's food reserve agency to settle its commercial debts. The government complied. When the crisis in food production turned into a famine in 2001–2002, there were hardly any reserves left to rush to the countryside. About 1,500 people perished.[41] The IMF, however, was unrepentant; in fact, it suspended its disbursements on an adjustment program with the government on the grounds that "the parastatal sector will continue to pose risks to the successful implementation of the 2002/03 budget. Government interventions in the food and other agricultural markets . . . crowd out more productive spending."[42]

When an even worse food crisis developed in 2005, the government had finally had enough of the Bank's and the IMF's institutionalized stupidity. Bingu wa Mutharika, then newly elected president, who had been an employee of the World Bank in the '70s, reintroduced the fertilizer subsidy program, enabling 1.7 million households—or 60 percent of Malawi's farmers—to buy a 50 kilogram bag of fertilizer at a quarter of the retail price and seeds at a discount. The results: bumper harvests for three years in a row, a surplus of one million tons of maize, and the country transformed into a supplier of corn to other countries in southern Africa.[43]

But the World Bank, like its sister agency, still stubbornly clung to the discredited doctrine. As the Bank's country director told the Toronto *Globe and Mail*, "All those farmers who begged, borrowed, and stole to buy extra fertilizer last year are now looking at that decision and rethinking it. The lower the maize price, the better for food security but worse for market development."[44]

Fleeing Failure

Malawi's defiance of the World Bank would probably have been an act of heroic but futile resistance a decade ago. The environment is different today. Owing to the absence of any clear case of success, structural adjustment has been widely discredited throughout Africa. Even some donor governments that used to subscribe to it have distanced themselves from the Bank, the most prominent case being the official British aid agency, the Department for International Development (DFID), which co-funded the latest subsidized fertilizer program in Malawi.[45] These institutions may be trying to shore up their eroding influence in the continent at a time when Chinese aid is emerging as an alternative to World Bank, IMF, and Western government aid programs with all the strings they have attached.

The FAO, usually subservient to the Bank, went out of its way to support the Malawi government's approach, giving President Mutharika the organization's highest award, the Agricola Model, for bringing about "a true food security success story in Africa."[46]

Beyond Africa, even former supporters of adjustment, like the International Food Policy Research Institute (IFPRI) in Washington and the rabidly neoliberal *Economist* magazine acknowledged that the state's abdication from agriculture was a mistake. In a recent commentary on the rise of food prices, for instance, IFPRI asserted that "rural investments have been sorely neglected in recent decades," and said that it was time for "developing country governments [to] increase their medium-and long-term investments in agricultural research and extension, rural infrastructure, and market access for small farmers."[47] At the same time, the Bank and IMF's espousal of free trade came under attack from the heart of the economics establishment itself, with a panel of luminaries headed by Princeton's Angus Deaton accusing the Bank's research department of being biased and "selective" in its research and presentation of data.[48] As the old saying goes, success has a thousand parents and failure is an orphan.

Admitting Failure

One of the harshest critics was the World Bank's own Independent Evaluation Group (IEG). The "biggest shortcoming," asserted the IEG, was that "the reform process had limited impact on food production," and the key cause of this, contrary to the Bank's expectations, was that in "most reforming countries the private sector did not step in to fill the vacuum when the public sector withdrew."[49]

The 2007 IEG Report is a litany of the costly failures of structural adjustment in the countryside.

In Kenya, the IEG noted "the failure of the Bank and borrower to focus sufficiently on the capacity of the private sector to pick up the roles left by divestiture . . . [given] the poorly developed trader and storage network."[50]

In Senegal, the Bank failed to study the distributional consequences of liberalization for poor farmers. Moreover, "achievement of the full benefits of the process required active government and donor support to develop and integrate markets, not simply 'liberalize' them. This meant attention to the development of infrastructure to ensure coordinated and sustainable systems of input delivery, farm finance, and reliable output markets, not simply trusting the market to take over."[51]

In Cameroon, the Bank-imposed price liberalization—a 40 percent cut in the official wholesale price of coffee—at a time of historically low world prices resulted in extremely low farm gate prices, so that "many farmers did not even harvest their coffee." At the same time, the elimination of state subsidies for fertilizer and pesticides dramatically reduced supplies of these inputs; the "inadequately developed private sector" was in no position to fill the gap. The result was a "significant depreciation of farmers' tree stock" that prevented farmers from responding robustly when prices rose. The IEG concluded that the overall result of structural adjustment was to "seriously handicap Cameroon's smallholder export sector."[52]

In a classic example of softening harsh criticism by using another's words, the IEG quoted the African academic Tshikala Tshibaka's comprehensive assessment of the privatization process supported under Bank projects:

> Little attempt was made to identify functions that are best performed by government agencies and those that are best handled by the private sector or to assess the private sector base in each country concerned. The failure to examine these and other related key questions has made it difficult for the designers of the structural adjustment reforms to propose appropriate policy measures and actions that could help strengthen the development of the private sector in order to enable it to effectively handle various functions that were previously carried out by parastatals in the economy.[53]

In another unsparing critique, Benno Ndulu underlined the role of state divestiture in creating "huge infrastructure gaps relative to needs in the region and compared to other developing regions. It is estimated that Sub-Saharan African countries need $18 billion a year in infrastructure financing in order to achieve the much higher 7 percent economic growth needed to halve extreme poverty in the region by 2015 . . ."[54]

Unable to deny the obvious, the Bank has finally acknowledged that the whole structural adjustment enterprise was a mistake, though it smuggled this concession into the middle of the *2008 World Development Report,* perhaps in the hope that it would not attract too much attention. Nevertheless, it was a damning admission:

> Structural adjustment in the 1980s dismantled the elaborate system of public agencies that provided farmers with access to land, credit, insurance inputs, and cooperative organization. The expectation was that removing the state would free the market for private actors to take over these functions—

reducing their costs, improving their quality, and eliminating their regressive bias. Too often, that didn't happen. In some places, the state's withdrawal was tentative at best, limiting private entry. Elsewhere, the private sector emerged only slowly and partially—mainly serving commercial farmers but leaving smallholders exposed to extensive market failures, high transaction costs and risks, and service gaps. Incomplete markets and institutional gaps impose huge costs in forgone growth and welfare losses for smallholders, threatening their competitiveness and, in many cases, their survival.[55]

Another Grand Strategy for Africa?

The acknowledgment of strategic mistakes in the promotion of structural adjustment has not prevented the World Bank from prescribing another grand strategy for Africa. Carefully analyzing the *World Development Report 2008*, Kjell Havnevik and his associates see the new World Bank paradigm for African agriculture as one based on the rapid development of contract and corporate farming. Smallholders are seen as largely noncompetitive, and the thrust of agricultural policy is to facilitate their conversion into large-scale contract farmers or into workers for corporate farms. WDR 2008, in short, "is recommending global capital's destruction of an independent smallholder agricultural sector."[56]

Here the Bank's approach ties in with that advocated by Paul Collier with much franker language than the Bank's: to quit romanticizing peasant agriculture and generalize Brazilian-type corporate agriculture to raise agricultural productivity quickly.[57] The Bank is silent about the Second Green Revolution based on genetically engineered seeds promoted by Collier, but this silence is likely to be tactical given the strong opposition to the use of genetically modified seeds in Africa at this point.[58]

But what of the millions of African peasants who will be displaced by large-scale agrarian capitalism? Here it is worth quoting in full Havnevik and his associates' deconstruction of the World Bank's solution:

> African smallholders have a "loser" status in the WDR 2008, but the World Bank appreciates that allowing the global market to fully decimate African peasant agriculture would spell political and human disaster in the weak African national economies where farmers' only option is to join over-crowded rural and urban informal sectors where average levels of capitalization, skills, and productivity are exceptionally low. Thus the African countryside of the future is in effect likely to be relegated to a large "holding ground" to ensure basic welfare of the rural population and provide labor for other sectors of the economy as and when needed.

In what the authors see as a major departure from the previous World Bank policy of indiscriminately promoting the commodification of land, the Bank now supports "evolutionary land tenure, seeing customary tenure as central for ensuring the poor's security" in selected rural reserves as capitalist relations transform the surrounding countryside. Havnevik continues:

> In other words, those left in the countryside live on tribal communal "holding grounds," akin to the Bantustans of the apartheid of South African history, eking out an existence on the basis of exceptionally low-yielding, uncapitalized agriculture. Like the Bantustans, these holding grounds could function as labour reserves for the mainstream national economy and would most likely be based on conservative tribal customary legal frameworks not only with respect to land but in a wide array of other spheres as well.

The authors conclude: "It is indeed an irony that such a possibility resurfaces little more than a decade after South Africa

managed to rid itself of this 'separate and unequal' model of
rural exploitation in the name of development."[59]

Conclusion

As a continent that imports some 25 percent of the food it
consumes, Africa has been at the center of the international food
price crisis. Lost in the call for a New Green Revolution based
on biotechnology to relieve the continent's food deficit are the
reasons for Africa's predicament.

As in Mexico and the Philippines, structural adjustment,
with its gutting of government budgets, especially the drastic
reduction or elimination of fertilizer subsidies, was the key
factor that turned relatively underpopulated Africa from a net
food exporter in the 1960s to the chronic net food importer
it is today. The aim of adjustment in Africa, as elsewhere,
was to make the continent's economies more efficient while
at the same time pushing them to export-oriented agricultural
production to acquire the foreign exchange necessary to service
their burgeoning foreign debts.

This doctrinaire solution, applied with the World Bank and
the IMF micromanaging the process, created instead more
poverty and more inequality, which is destroying the continent's
agricultural and industrial productive capacity. In Malawi, it
led to famine, which was only banished when the country's
government reinstituted fertilizer subsidies.

The World Bank now admits that by pushing for the
defunding of government programs, its policies helped erode
the productive capacity of the agriculture. Rather than allow
Africans to come out with indigenous solutions to the continent's
agrarian crisis, however, the Bank is currently promoting a
new development strategy relying on large-scale corporate
agriculture while creating "protected" reserves for marginalized
populations to carry on with the smallholder and communal
agriculture practices that the Bank considers obsolete.

Chapter 5

Peasants, the Party, and Agrarian Crisis in China

In one recent posting at a Chinese academic site, a commenter wrote: "I don't think it is a 'boast' . . . that China feeds about 20 percent of world population [on] 8 percent of world land . . . and remains more than 90 percent self-reliant."[1]

Who Will Feed China? Myths and Realities

Indeed, the worst fears fanned by Lester Brown's 1995 book *Who Will Feed China?* have turned out to be science fiction so far.[2] Claims during the 2006–2008 food crisis that increased demand for food in China and India was a key factor in the sharp rise in prices have been shown to be without much substance.[3] China imports only small amounts of high-grade rice, small amounts of wheat, and no corn. Indeed, not only has the country maintained self-sufficiency in basic grains; until 2008, it had been a net food exporter for three decades, becoming three years ago the world's fourth biggest exporter. An approving article that appeared in *Amber Waves*, a publication of the US Department of Agriculture, commented that "China dominates world markets in a variety of product areas, including garlic, apples, apple juice, mandarin oranges, farm-raised shrimp, and vegetables. At times, it seems that China has suspended the law of scarcity by boosting production in many sectors and selling at low prices without having to sacrifice production in other sectors."[4]

When Lester Brown visited Beijing early in June 2008, he expressed apprehension, not over a China that was dependent on global markets to feed itself, but over China's imposing taxes on rice and other grain exports to other developing countries.

Brown got one trend right, however, and that was the increased "meatification" of the Chinese diet. China has become the world's leading importer of soybeans for cattle feed, with some of the consequences that Brown warned about. During the decade 1994 to 2004, world trade in soybeans doubled, and 70 percent of the global increase in exports went to China, where meat production shot up from 45 million to 74 million tons. Agribusiness in Brazil and Argentina rushed to fill the demand, with the two countries providing more than two-thirds of the increased global exports of soybeans.[5] The consequences were detailed by the World Bank:

> Rapid growth in exports from Argentina and Brazil has been supported by bringing new land under cultivation, often at the expense of forests and woodlands. In the northern Salta region of Argentina, half the area under soybean cultivation in 2002/03 was previously covered by natural vegetation. Much of this included the highly threatened *Chaco* ecosystem. In Brazil the states of Goias, Mato Grosso, and Mato Grosso do Sul doubled the area under soybean cultivation between 1999/2000 and 2004/05 by planting an additional 54,000 square kilometers—an area larger than Costa Rica—much of it displacing ecologically important savanna woodland (*cerrado*) and forest. Because trees are being burned to create open land in the frontier states of Para, Mato Grosso, Acre, and Rondonia, Brazil has become one of the world's largest emitters of greenhouse gases.[6]

The World Bank could not, however, pretend it did not have a role in this, for its prescription of rapid export-oriented industrialization has been faithfully followed by China, down to the creation of an urban middle class who would spur trade with new demand brought about by lifestyle changes, including a more meat-heavy diet. In fact, getting China to be less self-sufficient and more dependent on international trade was a good thing from the Bank's neoclassical perspective, this would result in overall greater "efficiency" for the global economy.

Ever since the first years of the People's Republic of China in the 1950s, the government has pursued a policy of food self-reliance. That goal is now under threat for several reasons.

First, as noted above, the transition from a largely cereal diet to greater meat dependency may necessitate ever greater imports not only of soybeans but of other grains as well for animal feed.

Second, China's liberalization of its agricultural trade, a thrust represented by its joining the World Trade Organization in 2001, is certain to have a negative impact on domestic food production and will definitely increase food dependency on the global market. Chinese demand may not have played a significant role in the 2007–2008 food price hikes, but it may in future hikes. Most studies of China's WTO membership conclude that it will be a net loser. One of the most comprehensive studies asserted that the WTO-mandated agricultural and trade reforms would "result in substantial negative impacts across the sector and a worsening of food security in the sense of reduced access to income."[7] Less self-sufficiency in many commodities, including key grains, was certain,[8] as was loss of work and income for "hundreds of millions of farmers."[9] Another study noted that "an estimated six million people will leave their farm jobs" and "real farm wages . . . will decline."[10] A study of global trade liberalization found that the farmers who "would lose most are in China, with potential losses of $75 billion."[11] Internal inequality would also increase, with one World Bank study straightforwardly asserting that China's "basic accession commitments to reduce agricultural import protection and eliminate agricultural subsidies will make those farm households dependent on agriculture worse off relative to urban households."[12]

China's impact on the global economy as a competitor for insufficient commodities—the great worry of Brown and other environmentalists—did not enter into the calculations of World Bank economists supporting China's entry into the WTO. They were confident that supply would continually expand to meet rising demand, an assumption that events over the previous few years had already proved wrong.

Third, production was beginning to hit ecological limits. Expanded use of fertilizer brought about decreasing returns as soil quality eroded. Meanwhile, water shortages, particularly in the North China Plain, which produces a large share of China's wheat, corn, and other heavily irrigated crops, have worsened. Agriculture now finds itself competing with nonfarm users. Whereas in 1980 industrial and domestic consumers used only 13 percent of the water consumed in China, with agriculture accounting for the rest, by 2000 agriculture's share had gone down to two-thirds and industry and domestic users had moved up to one third. Already, "on the productive North China Plain, water diversions for human use are well over 60 percent of renewable water resources."[13] Water scarcity contributed to grain production in northern China falling by 50 million tons between 1998 and 2004.[14]

Fourth, there was a decrease in spending for agricultural infrastructure and technological research. Chinese agricultural research has been declining since the 1980s, and the country's public investment for agricultural research is now one of the lowest—in relation to GDP—in the world. Investment for agrotechnological extension has also dropped.[15] Water conservation projects are hugely important given the critical water situation. However, in recent years, investment in water conservancy projects only accounted for about one percent of the country's total capital investment in infrastructure, and funds allocated for flood-control projects made up only 6 percent of the state's total expenditure. Poor maintenance of irrigation and flood control facilities contributed to China's relatively low average per-hectare crop yield and agricultural productivity.[16]

Fifth, urban residential, commercial, and industrial agglomerations were rapidly taking over the land. Between 1984 and 1989, farmland decreased at a rate of 640,000 hectares a year, with a record one million hectares taken out of agricultural production in 1985. Between 1990 and 1997, the average yearly loss of farmland was slightly up, at 657,000 hectares a year, with another million taken out in 1996. Since then, the situation has gotten even worse, with 4.1 million hectares taken out of cultivation between 1996 and 2002. In other words, cultivated land between 1996 and 2002 fell from 130 million to 125.9 million, or a net loss of 3.16 percent in just seven years.[17]

These disturbing processes reflected a policy of transferring agricultural surplus to industry, extracting value created by the countryside to subsidize rapid industrialization in the cities. The policy is well entrenched, predating the reform era that began in 1978, and has been enforced through prices that favor industrial products, heavy taxation of farmers, and prioritization of urban-industrial development in government spending. One estimate of the transfer of agricultural surplus to the industrial and, more broadly, urban sectors is an astounding 562.7 billion yuan between 1978 and 1996.[18] Not surprisingly, except for the period 1978 to 1985, when the household responsibility system (discussed below) and the first rural market reforms were implemented, the rate of growth of agricultural production has lagged behind that of industry, the rate of the rise in agricultural production has outstripped that of the rise of farmers' income, and a troubling gap has opened up and widened between urban and rural incomes. By the mid-1990s, even as official statistics proclaimed that the poverty rate had declined to less than 10 percent of the rural population, commentators began to speak about a "floating population" of 100 million poverty-stricken peasants migrating to the cities to offer themselves as dirt–cheap labor in the privileged cities of south and eastern China.

Food, poverty, prosperity, stability, and crises have been intertwined with the fate of the peasantry in China, perhaps more than in most other countries. Whereas the United States saw its farm populations decline from 60 percent in 1900 to less than 1 percent today with little social upheaval, macroecononomic transformation in China has always been accompanied by the specter if not the reality of peasant unrest, and never more so than today.

A Troubled Relationship

It is sadly ironic that the peasantry has gotten the short end of the stick of development, since the Chinese Communist Party, after all, came to power on the backs of the peasantry, with the promise of bringing about agrarian prosperity.

Political sociologists have sometimes described the Chinese Revolution as the product of an alliance between middle-class intellectuals and the peasantry. In his innovative revision of Marxist-Leninist theory, Mao Zedong transformed the peasantry, a class disdained by Marx, into the "main force" of his antifeudal, anti–imperialist revolution. Translated into practice by the Communist Party, which was led and dominated by the revolutionary intelligentsia, this reformulation underpinned the Communist triumph in 1949.

But the relationship between the Communist Party (CPC) and the Chinese peasantry has never been an easy one. Indeed, it may be more aptly described as tumultuous.

A Receding Vision

The vision of agricultural transformation that won for the Communists the support of millions of peasants—a countryside where land seized from landlords would be tilled by millions of small owner-cultivators—remained precisely that: a vision. The party requisitioned all grain surpluses above the peasants' survival needs to fulfill Mao's industry-first policy. Peasant freedom was curtailed when production was collectivized in the mid-'50s. Then during the Great Leap Forward, from 1958 to 1961, to spur production to support Mao's super-industrialization drive, the party herded peasants into communes—of which there were 26,000-plus in the whole of China—where their lives revolved around hard labor. According to one riveting account of those years, party cadres were engaged in micromanaging production, keeping peasants "penned inside their villages," and preventing them from "stealing" their own harvest.[19]

After the disaster that overtook this social experiment, in which some 30 million people, mainly peasants, died from malnourishment and starvation, the balance of power in the struggle over the surplus shifted to the peasantry. Requisitioning targets were lowered, and, as Jung Chang and Jon Halliday note, "in many places, peasants were allowed to lease land from the commune, and effectively were able to return to being individual farmers. This alleviated starvation and motivated productivity."[20]

Peasants and the Great Proletarian Cultural Revolution

Specialists studying rural China debate the impact on the peasantry of the next great event, the Cultural Revolution. To Chen Guidi and Wu Chantao, authors of a compassionate chronicle of peasant suffering under party rule, the Cultural Revolution was a "disaster" for the peasantry: "A peasant would be accused of 'taking the capitalist road' if his household kept two chickens or planted a few vegetables for the market."[21] In contrast, for Roderick MacFarquhar and Michael Schoenhals, the Cultural Revolution, which began in earnest in 1966, spelled relief for the peasantry. With the party self-destructing

as Mao purged "capitalist roaders" he saw ensconced at all levels
of the party, the ability of the authorities to requisition grain
was eroded. As they describe it in their magisterial *Mao's Last
Revolution*,

> To be left alone was what many peasants secretly wished
> for, and when the state's tax collectors failed to show up on
> time or in force because they were involved in struggles, the
> peasants were content. In parts of rural China, an unintended
> by-product of a dysfunctional state bureaucracy was hailed
> as a great, newborn thing. In Shehong county, Sichuan,
> peasants were told that "Cultural Revolution means no more
> grain deliveries to the state!"[22]

Racked by factional infighting, party and government operatives
could not collect grain taxes on time or in full. Indeed, in
the two subprovincial regions of Suzhou and Zhenjiang, in
Jiangsu, "agricultural taxes equal to 200 million jin [100 million
kilograms] of grain were simply never collected. The situation
was similar in the subprovincial regions of Enshi and Xiangyang,
in Hubei, where agricultural taxes equal to 60 million jin
remained uncollected."[23]

Not surprisingly, from 214 million tons in 1966, production
rose throughout the Cultural Revolution, reaching 286
million tons in 1976. With the disruption in collection and
transportation, added production did not benefit the cities but
was absorbed by peasant households. But greater production
was not the only consequence of the relaxation of the party's
iron hand. The Cultural Revolution years saw, in some parts of
rural China, "a resurgence of household-based farming, which
the peasants preferred. In Yibin prefecture, Sichuan, 8,355 of
49,349 production teams were by 1969 redistributing fields to
individual households, contracting production out to individual
households . . . allowing the 'seizure of the collective economy'
by private interests."[24]

The "Golden Age"

The shift in power toward the peasantry appeared to be consolidated with the reforms initiated by Deng Xiaoping after the death of Mao in 1976. The peasants wanted an end to the communes, and Deng and his reformers obliged them by introducing the "household–contract responsibility system." Under this scheme, each household was given a piece of land to farm. Of what it produced, the household was allowed to retain what was left over after selling to the state a fixed proportion at a state-determined price, or by simply paying a tax in cash. The rest it could consume or sell on the market.

There is consensus among China specialists that these were the golden years of the peasantry. The sense of great expectations is evoked by Chen Guidi and Wu Chuntao in their report on agrarian conflicts in Anhui Province:

> When the Cultural Revolution was finally brought to a halt, following Mao's death in 1976, the household–contract system was tried out in Anhui Province and proved a great success. The lethargy of the previous years was gone. One could frequently see three generations of a family working together under one of those contracts, looking toward a better life. The reform saw a sustained 15 percent increase of per capita income for the years 1978 to 1984. It was the years of recovery.[25]

Other accounts of the period confirm that this was indeed the one time when the peasantry truly benefited from reform, but that at the same time, the reform contained the seeds of what would later become one of the main problems plaguing the countryside:

> It must be noted that of all of China's reform stages, this phase of reforms showed the most substantial decrease in poverty.

According to Chinese official estimates, between 1978 and 1984 rural poverty declined from 33 percent to 11 percent of the population. In actual numbers it meant that the number of people living in poverty declined from 260 million to 89 million in a matter of six years. This was and is an unprecedented achievement in the history of development. At the same time, however, there was a considerable increase in income inequality due to decollectivization and the dismantling of the egalitarian redistribution mechanisms embedded in the communes. Inequality as measured by the Gini coefficient grew from 0.21 in 1978 to 0.26 in 1984.[26]

The rural reform has been characterized as a "big-bang," the consequences of which were felt throughout the economy. Minxin Pei notes that the surpluses generated by the reform "allowed rural governments to invest in new manufacturing businesses, which eventually became a critical source of public finance."[27]

Those who have studied the economic transformation of Taiwan are struck by the similarity between the 1978–84 reform period in China and the 1950s in Taiwan, when radical land reform created and consolidated former tenants into a prospering owner-cultivator class, whose demand for farm implements and other manufactures triggered and sustained the island's early import-substitution industrialization, geared toward reducing its dependency on foreign products.

The Great Reversal

But as in Taiwan, the golden age of the peasantry came to an end, and the cause was identical: the adoption of a strategy of urban-centered, export-oriented industrialization based on rapid integration into the global capitalist economy. This strategy, which was launched at the 12th National Party Congress, in 1984, was essentially one that built the urban industrial economy on "the shoulders of peasants," as Chen and Wu put it.[28] Primitive capital accumulation was achieved mainly by heavily taxing peasant surpluses. And as in the Great Leap Forward, the party organization in the countryside played the role of overseer in the new strategy.

The consequences of this urban–oriented development strategy were stark. Peasant income, which had grown by 15.2 percent a year from 1978 to 1984, dropped by 2.8 percent a year from 1986 to 1991. Some recovery occurred in the early 1990s, but stagnation of rural income marked the latter part of the decade. In contrast, urban income, already higher than that of peasants in the mid-'80s, was, on average, six times the income of peasants by 2000.

The stagnation of rural income was caused by the rising costs of agricultural inputs, falling prices for agricultural products, and increased taxes, all of which operated to transfer income from the countryside to the city. But the main mechanism for the extraction of surplus from the peasantry was the third factor, taxation. Taxes on 149 agricultural products were levied on the peasants by central state agencies by 1991, but this proved to be but part of a much bigger bite, as the lower levels of government began to levy their own taxes, fees, and charges. Currently, the various tiers of rural government impose a total of 269 types of tax, along with all sorts of often arbitrarily imposed administrative charges.[29]

Taxes and fees were not supposed to exceed 5 percent of a farmer's income, but the actual amount was often much greater; some Ministry of Agriculture surveys reported that the peasant tax burden was 15 percent—three times the official national limit.[30]

Expanded taxation would perhaps have been bearable had peasants experienced returns such as improved public health and education and more agricultural infrastructure. In the absence of such tangible benefits, the peasants saw their incomes as subsidizing what Chen and Wu describe as the "monstrous growth of the bureaucracy and the metastasizing number of officials" who seemed to have no other function than to extract more and more from them.

Aside from being subjected to higher input prices, lower prices for their goods, and more intensive taxation, peasants have borne the brunt of the urban-industrial focus of economic strategy in other ways. According to one report, "40 million peasants have been forced off their land to make way for roads, airports, dams, factories, and other public and private investments, with an additional two million to be displaced each year."[31] Other researchers cited a much higher figure of 70 million households, meaning that, calculating 4.5 persons per household, by 2004 as many as 315 million people may have been displaced by land grabs.[32]

The Threat of Trade Liberalization

But the impact of all these forces may yet be dwarfed by that of China's commitment to eliminate agricultural quotas and reduce tariffs, made when it joined the World Trade Organization. And the cost of admission for China is proving to be huge and disproportionate:

> The challenge of managing the farm sector has grown with China's WTO commitments in agriculture, which are more far-reaching than those of other developing countries and in certain respects exceed those of high-income countries. The Chinese government agreed to reduce tariffs and institute other policies that meaningfully increase market access; accepted tight restrictions on the use of agricultural subsidies; and pledged to eliminate all agricultural export subsidies— commitments that go far beyond those made by other participants in the Uruguay Round negotiations that led to the WTO's creation.[33]

Indeed, the government slashed its average agricultural tariff from 54 percent to 15.3 percent, compared with the world average of 62 percent, prompting the commerce minister to boast (or complain): "Not a single member in the WTO history has made such a huge cut [in tariffs] in such a short period of time."[34]

The WTO deal reflects China's current priorities. If the party leadership has chosen to put at risk large sections of its agriculture, such as soybeans and cotton, this is because the party wants to open up or keep open global markets for its industrial exports.[35] The social consequences of this trade-off are still to be fully felt, but the immediate effects were alarming. In 2004, after years of being a net food exporter, China registered a deficit in its agricultural trade. Cotton imports had skyrocketed from 11,300 tons in 2001 to 1.98 million tons in 2004, a 175-fold increase. Chinese sugarcane, soybean, and most of all, cotton farmers were devastated.[36] In 2005, according to Oxfam Hong Kong, imports of cheap US cotton resulted in a loss of $208 million in income for Chinese peasants, along with 720,000 jobs.[37] Trade liberalization is also likely to have contributed to the dramatic slowdown in poverty reduction in the period between 2000 and 2004.

The New Overlords?

Corruption, which multiplied among party cadres in the "to get rich is glorious" climate of the post-Mao era, was kerosene poured on the already volatile relationship between peasants and the party, and when local party officials were seen abetting or coddling mafia elements—many of them party members themselves—peasant anger at people who now seemed to be their new feudal overlords intensified. Chen and Wu's book is a dismal chronicle of this transformation of the party from dedicated and respected cadres to a veritable rural ruling class lording it over the peasants. It is worth reproducing in full their description of how this class exercises one of its "privileges":

> The fact of the matter is the vast countryside of China has become a gourmand's paradise. Like a cloud of locusts, officials with their appetites in tow descend on the countryside and are infinitely inventive in coming up with excuses to eat and drink: dinners for inspectors, dinners for conferences, dinners for rural poverty relief; dine if you can afford it, and dine if you can't; dine on credit, dine on loan; keep the dinners going from one year's end to another, from one month's end to another, from morning till night; enjoy dinners when you take office and when you leave office.
>
> A popular saying about eating and drinking at public expense runs "There's nothing to be gained by not eating since it's free; so why not eat?" To eat free has become a sign of status, an index of position. The quality of a dinner may determine whether or not a project is approved or a deal clinched, or whether a promotion is in the works. It has become part of political culture.[38]

With the prevalence of such practices, it is not surprising that protests have multiplied. From 8,700 in 1993, the number of "mass group incidents," as the Ministry of Public Security calls them, increased to 87,000 in 2005, most of them in the countryside. Moreover, the incidents are growing in average size from ten or fewer participants in the mid-1990s to fifty-two people per incident in 2004.[39]

A widespread form of protest is tax resistance. Minxin Pei claims that in Xinjiang in 2001, tax resistance was said to be prevalent in 40 percent of the villages surveyed. In that same survey, about 70 percent of village cadres felt that collecting fees was the most difficult task. The use of police to force peasants to pay up is common, as documented by Chen and Wu. And in many areas, party officials, according to Pei, "recruited thugs as their collection agents. Such a practice has resulted in illegal imprisonment, torture, and the deaths of peasants who were unable to pay."[40]

Can the CCP regain peasant confidence?

The relations between the party and the peasantry are perhaps at their nadir today. Throughout their turbulent seventy-five-year relationship, the party has always been able to bounce back and regain the peasantry's confidence after disastrous policies, such as the Great Leap Forward and the Cultural Revolution. Will it be able to do so once more?

Emulating the ancient tradition of appealing to the imperial center to curb the depredations of local lords, peasants have sent delegations to Beijing to lodge complaints against local authorities. Yet positive responses from the center—prosecution of corrupt cadres and otherwise reining in abusive practices—are erratic and inconsistent. As Chen and Wu's accounts make clear, certain people in the party do care about peasants and have taken up the cudgels for them.[41] The problem is that inertia, corruption, bureaucracy, and indifference militate against any serious internal party reform.

Might some sort of ideological renewal reinvigorate the old relationship? Having jettisoned its socialist vision—even as it has kept the socialist rhetoric—the party has had to construct an alternative ideology of legitimation for the era of rapid capitalist development. Dennis Lynch describes this alternative ideology as a "CCP-led return to national greatness" through the achievement of "comprehensive national power" and a "recentering of Chinese civilization."[42] The new, expanding urban middle classes that have benefited from the export-led, urban-centered development of the past two decades have certainly been susceptible to this idea. It is, however, unlikely that this new vision has significant appeal to the peasants, migrant workers, and laid-off workers from state owned enterprises who have borne the costs of China's high-speed industrialization.

What about the much-touted village elections? Not even the harshest of China's critics can deny that there is strong and growing competition in village elections, which were introduced in the 1980s. The role that rural democratization, limited though it may currently be, can play in revitalizing the relationship between party and peasants must not be underestimated. But while the elections have allowed rural people some measure of control over local government, all too often they have been manipulated by party and national government officials. Moreover, the CCP has blocked elections above the village level, so that the party continues to fill township and country level offices with its cadres.[43]

In looking for "a way out" of the current impasse, Chen and Wu cite the views of a prominent rural specialist, Yu Jianrong, of the Agricultural Research Center at Central China University: "Yu's solution is to rally the peasants to form their own organization and replace the current local bureaucracy by peasants' self rule. Yu proposed that only a network of peasant organizations could truly represent the peasants' interests and needs and communicate them in an orderly way and prevent and ameliorate confrontations and conflicts."[44]

Yu's solution may sound utopian, but it does reflect really dismal-seeming prospects for the relations between the party and the peasantry. This puts a pall of uncertainty over the future of China, despite the country's double-digit growth rates. It is one of the greatest ironies of contemporary history that the Chinese Communist Party, after having led the Chinese people to victory against imperialism and bringing about what is undoubtedly an economic miracle, should now find itself alienated from what used to be its primary and, arguably, its most important constituency because of its strategic decision to ride the tiger of global capitalism while retaining authoritarian controls. Few analysts see peasant discontent as a serious challenge to the party's rule in the short and medium term, but a lack of legitimacy among such a great part of the population can ultimately have only disastrous consequences.

Agrarian Reform or Capitalist Transformation?

In the past few years, the contradictions between food security needs and the priority placed on export-oriented industrialization have moved the party more and more to two solutions: trade liberalization and loosening of the property regime. The consequences of the trade liberalization have already been detailed. Loosening the property regime involves easing public controls over land in order to move toward a full-fledged private property regime. The idea is to allow the sale of land rights (the creation of a land market) so that the most efficient producers can expand their holdings. In the euphemistic words of a US Department of Agriculture publication, "China is strengthening farmers' rights—although stopping short of allowing full ownership of land—so farmers can rent land, consolidate their holdings, and achieve efficiencies in size and scale."[45]

Previous liberalization of land rights after the milestone household-responsibility system included the passage of the Agricultural Lease Law in 2003, which curtailed the village authorities' ability to reallocate land and gave farmers the right to inherit and sell leaseholds for arable land for thirty years. This paved the way for a new agricultural policy thrust approved by the CCP Central Committee in late October 2008, in the midst of the financial crisis, that positively encouraged the leasing and consolidation of land:

We should strengthen the market of land use right circulation. Farmers are allowed to circulate the right of contracted land in the manner of transfer, lease, swap, sub-contract, or stock shares to develop to optimum scale-management. Family farms and large-scale farmers should be developed when and where the condition is favorable.[46]

With the buying and selling of rights to use land for up to thirty years, private property in land was essentially reestablished in China. In talking about "family farms" and "large-scale farmers," the party was, in fact, endorsing a capitalist development path to supplant one that had been based on small-scale peasant agriculture. As one partisan of the new policy argued, "The reform would create both an economy of scale—raising efficiency and lowering agricultural production costs—but also resolve the problem of idle land left by migrants to the cities."[47]

Despite the assurance by the party that it was institutionalizing the peasants' rights to land, many saw that the new policy would legalize the process of illegal land grabbing that had been occurring on a wide scale. This would, they warned, "create a few landlords and many landless farmers who will have no means of living."[48] Given the turbulent transformation of the countryside by the full-scale unleashing of capitalist relations of production in other countries, these fears were not misplaced.

Thus, sixty years after the peasant-based pro-socialist revolution, the CCP was abandoning its long-standing food self-sufficiency policy, exposing its population to the vagaries of the international agricultural market, and promoting the full-scale capitalist transformation of the countryside. With capitalist relations gathering strength in the countryside, food insecurity, land insecurity, and income inequalities are likely to increase.

Given China's massive weight in the international economy, these trends are likely to have a significant global impact. With WTO-related trade liberalization eroding China's productive capacity in agriculture, the country would now compete with other countries in a global economy increasingly hobbled by supply constraints created by structural adjustment programs and neoliberal reforms. This would result in a permanent upward thrust in food prices.

Today's deepening global economic crisis may counteract these trends, however. As of early 2009, twenty million workers had already been laid off because of falling demand in China's key export markets, and the government announced the creation of a $580-million plus stimulus package aimed at stoking domestic demand. Much of the money would be spent on infrastructure in the countryside. A simple countercyclical mechanism cannot, however, change overnight the structures of an export-oriented economy. Refocusing on the domestic market and the countryside would mean a fundamental policy shift, and the government would have to go against the interests, both local and foreign, that have congealed around the strategy of foreign-capital-dependent, export-oriented industrialization. At this writing it is not clear that it will have the courage to do so.

Conclusion

The rise in Chinese demand for food contributed little to the contemporary food price crisis. However, the "meatification" of the Chinese diet is posing a threat to the environment as large tracts of land in South America are converted to soybean plantations to provide fodder for Chinese livestock. At a time when climate change poses a mortal risk, the elimination of hundreds of hectares of forest serving as a critical planetary carbon sink is worrisome.

China has followed a policy of food self-sufficiency since the Communists came to power in 1949. Yet this policy is in danger of being eroded. One reason is the continuing subordination of agriculture to export-oriented industrialization. Surplus from the countryside has been channeled to industry through taxes and mechanisms of price discrimination against agricultural products. This bleeding of the countryside has resulted in rising inequality between the rural and urban populations. Peasants are fleeing to the cities, where they serve as the "floating population" of cheap labor that has been the engine of China's rapid industrialization.

Another reason for the erosion of self-sufficiency is the liberalization of agricultural trade mandated by China's admission to the World Trade Organization. With the displacement of cotton, sugar, and soybean farmers, China will become more and more dependent on the international market for food, which will likely lead to rising food prices.

The relationship between the peasantry and the Communist Party is experiencing renewed stresses in this climate of agricultural crisis. The party came to power on the backs of the peasantry, but except for the period from 1978 to 1984, when agricultural reforms led to peasant prosperity, the countryside has been made to serve as the key engine of capital accumulation for export-oriented industry. In recent years, rural discontent has spilled over into social protest, both violent and in the form of tax evasion.

The land issue is another flashpoint. Party officials have been involved in illegal landgrabs totaling millions of hectares. Also, there is afoot a major effort to transform the land tenure system to allow for the easier buying and selling of rights to use land, which, in the opinion of many, would be a step toward full-fledged private property and facilitate the emergence of large-scale capitalist agriculture.

With the global economic implosion reducing demand in China's main markets, including the United States, the government is trying to stimulate domestic demand, partly by pouring investment into the countryside. This countercyclical strategy, however, will be limited in its impact unless it is accompanied by a significant redistribution to the countryside of income and resources from the urban beneficiaries of export-oriented industrialization.

Chapter 6

Agrofuels and Food Insecurity*

On July 3, 2008, the *Guardian* came out with an exposé on a secret report made by a World Bank economist. The report claimed that US and EU agrofuels policies were responsible for three quarters of the 140 percent increase in food prices between 2002 and February 2008.[1] This figure was significantly higher than the 3 percent previously reported by the US Department of Agriculture (USDA), Oxfam's estimate of around 30 percent, the IMF figure of 20 to 30 percent, and the Organisation for Economic Co-operation and Development's (OECD) 60 percent. The report's conclusion was straightforward:

> the most important factor [in the food price increases] was the large increase in biofuels production in the US and the EU. Without these increases, global wheat and maize stocks would not have declined appreciably, oilseed prices would not have tripled, and price increases due to other factors, such as droughts, would have been more moderate. Recent export bans and speculative activities would probably not have occurred because they were largely responses to rising prices.[2]

* This chapter could not have been written without the efforts, assistance and advice of Mara Baviera.

Completed as early as April 2008, the Mitchell report—named after the lead economist of the World Bank research team, Donald Mitchell—was allegedly suppressed by the World Bank out of fear of embarrassing former US president George Bush and his aggressive agrofuels policy.[3]

The term *agrofuels* refers mainly to ethanol and biodiesel being developed for use as transportation fuel. Agrofuels are renewable sources of energy made from biological materials. Ethanol is a widely used agrofuel made from crops high in sugar or starch. In Brazil, ethanol is made from sugarcane, while in the United States, corn serves as the feedstock. Biodiesel, produced from oils and fats, is another kind of agrofuel, one that is more commonly produced and consumed in Europe. *Biofuel* is the more commonly used term, because it has an environmentally benign connotation, but these fuels are hardly innocuous. Indeed, agrofuels contribute to global warming and certainly do not provide a solution to climate change. The climate agenda mainly serves as an excellent and convenient spin for the agrofuels regime already being built.

Agrofuels have been blamed for the food price increases of the past two years. They have certainly contributed to them, and this chapter brings together the evidence for this claim. However, their role has been to aggravate rather than cause the volatility of food prices. More central as root causes have been structural adjustment, free trade, and policies extracting surplus from agriculture for industrialization, all of which have destroyed or eroded the agricultural sector of many countries. No one factor can be pinpointed as the cause of the global food crisis. It is the confluence of these conditions that has made the contemporary food price crisis so threatening and difficult to solve.

Profiting from the Crisis:
Agrofuels in the United States

The United States is at the nexus of agrofuel production and the food crisis. This is hardly surprising, since over the past few years the Bush administration's generous support, made in the name of combating climate change, has made conversion of corn into agrofuel feedstock instead of food very profitable.

In January 2007, President Bush put the agrofuels agenda at the center of his final State of the Union address. Dubbing the program "20 in 10," Bush laid out plans to reduce American consumption of fossil fuels and dependence on oil imports through mandatory use of renewable energy, mainly in the form of agrofuels. Renewable sources should constitute a minimum of 20 percent of the energy portfolio in the transport sector within ten years—thus "20 in 10." His team estimated that this policy would result in a 10 percent cut in carbon emissions from automobiles by 2017.

In 2007, with the Bush administration's active lobbying, the US Congress passed the Energy Independence and Security Act for the promotion of agrofuels and the automobile-fuel industry. The act mandates the increase of agrofuels production by more than eightfold, from 4.7 billion gallons in 2007 to at least 36 billion gallons in 2022—unusually high standards that would mean significant changes in agricultural production. As of late 2007, there were 135 ethanol refineries in operation and 74 more being built or expanded.[4] Midwestern America saw itself slowly being transformed into a giant agrofuels factory. In 2008, about 30 percent of corn was allocated for ethanol, after rapid increases since 2006. Currently, the Environmental Protection Agency (EPA) in the United States is enforcing the implementation of renewable fuel standards. For the year 2009, refiners, importers, and blenders are required to obtain 10.21 percent of fuel from renewable sources. The triad of strict mandates and standards, import tariffs, and subsidies make for a strong agrofuels policy that is skewing the market in a negative direction, driving up the price of food, and harming the environment.

The Global Subsidies Initiative, a Geneva-based organization that monitors the agrofuel subsidy programs of different countries, estimates that under 2007 policies, federal, state, and municipal governments will be allocating more than $92 billion in subsidies from 2006 to 2012. Up to 88 percent of this amount goes to corn-based ethanol production in the form of tax credits to agrofuels blenders, market price support, and direct crop payments.[5] Not surprisingly, there are major problems associated with the US government's ethanol subsidies, the most important of which are the strong incentives to convert nonagricultural land for maize production and the fact that these subsidies benefit mainly corporate interests.

Under the so-called B99 program, the United States has been accused of dumping subsidized biodiesel in the EU market.[6] US biodiesel producers get a $1 per gallon subsidy for blending 99 percent biodiesel with 1 percent mineral diesel. According to one report:

> Around 1 million tonnes of B99 biodiesel are believed to have been 'dumped' by the US into the EU this year. About 10% of that consisted of biodiesel produced from palm plantations planted on rainforest in Southeast Asia, blended in the US and then sold on to the EU.[7]

Brazilian sugarcane-based ethanol is also facing competitive pressure from the heavy subsidization of the American agrofuels industry. Import tariffs on Brazilian ethanol amount to fifty-four cents per gallon. The South American variant is allegedly more energy efficient and cheaper to produce than the corn-based agrofuel made in the US, though, admittedly, self-interested Brazilian ethanol interests are among the voices making this claim.

Aggressively pushed by government and the agribusiness corporations, the exacerbation of the food crisis through land conversion is not the only problem with the highly subsidized US ethanol program. Ironically, the "green" fuel initiative is also harming the environment inside and outside the United States.

In Alabama and Iowa, biodiesel plants are polluting rivers and killing fish through grease and vegetable oil spills.[8]

Cargill, on its website, admits implicitly that profitability rather than environmental considerations will be the central criterion in its decision to go for agrofuels in a big way:

> High crude oil prices and government subsidies and policies encouraging the use of vegetable oils as fuel alternatives have driven increased global demand for using palm oil to create biodiesel. In July 2006, Malaysia and Indonesia announced they would set aside 40 percent of their annual palm output for biodiesel.
>
> While Cargill believes that biofuels have a meaningful role to play in helping meet global energy needs, the company also believes that the marketplace is the best place for such questions to be decided. Cargill will invest in biofuels and supply the biofuel market when and where it makes sense, including with palm oil.[9]

With an estimated $1 billion invested in ethanol and biodiesel,[10] it is very difficult to imagine the agribusiness giant seriously expressing concern over production processes harming the environment or having social costs.

Another large agribusiness corporation, Archer Daniels Midland (ADM), has been very active in lobbying for energy, trade, and environmental legislation favorable to agrofuels. In 2008, the corporation spent around $1 million in its lobbying efforts,[11] a tidy trade-off considering that agrofuels accounted for 19 percent of the company's profits.[12] ADM is setting up a palm oil-based biodiesel plant in Indonesia and a soybean-based plant in Brazil.

Agrofuels bring negative environmental impacts, fuel the food crisis, and have appalling social consequences particularly in plantations in the South (see below). They don't even make economic sense for society as a whole. So why does the ethanol program continue to be such a high priority?

American corporations such as Cargill, ADM, and Noble are throwing in large investments. Oil companies like British Petroleum and Mitsui are joining the fray. ExxonMobil has given Stanford University $100 million for agrofuels research. Chevron, which owns a biodiesel plant in Texas, is pouring money into Georgia Institute of Technology, the University of California, Davis, and Colorado universities to fund research.[13]

A report from the international NGO Grain identifies who is profiting and driving policy on agrofuels:

> There are the billionaires: George Soros, the hedge fund guru, owns ethanol/agribusiness operations in Brazil; Bill Gates owns one of the US's largest ethanol producers; Vinod Khosla, of Google fame, is a major investor in a range of agrofuel production and technology ventures; and Sir Richard Branson, owner of Virgin Group and now Virgin Fuels, has a growing portfolio of agrofuel investments. These titans of globalisation not only bring their vast fortunes to the agrofuel gold rush, but their heavy political clout as well.[14]

People are rushing into agrofuels because they perceive them as a future profit center, just like biotechnology in the 1980s. If one does not get in on the ground floor, one might be shut out of the bonanza later on. Silvia Ribeiro and Hope Shand make this point succinctly:

> Corporate concentration in agriculture has allowed a handful of powerful corporations to seize the agricultural research agenda, influence national and international trade and agricultural policy and engineer the acceptance of new

technologies as the "science-based" solution to maximizing food production. Although frequently promoted in the name of addressing the needs of the world's poor and hungry, the benefits of these technologies typically [accrue] to those who develop and control them.[15]

The EU's Foray into Agrofuels

Fuel consumption in the EU is different from that in the United States, as diesel has a significantly larger market share compared with gasoline. Hence, the agrofuels policy in the region is oriented more toward biodiesel production and importation as opposed to ethanol. In 2003, the European Commission issued a directive mandating the production and use of agrofuels by its twenty-seven member states. Targets were set at 5.75 percent of fuels by 2010. Various instruments and legislation in the member countries proliferated after the issuance of this directive. Different member states pursued various levels of compliance. Finland and Denmark, for example, set their national agrofuels targets lower than the 2 percent 2005 reference value mandated by the directive. Only Germany and Sweden complied with the 2 percent target. The main instruments used to promote domestic production are subsidies for energy crops, setting aside of land for agrofuel production, tax incentives, and high tariffs on imported ethanol.

A 2007 progress report issued by the Commission estimated that the 2010 targets are not likely to be achieved.[16] Production in the region will not suffice to meet the deadline, as the land required for biodiesel is extensive. The EU imports palm oil from Malaysia and Indonesia and ethanol from Brazil. Up to 58 percent of agrofuels in EU may have to be imported, mostly from developing countries.

The motivations for pursuing an agrofuel policy in the EU are allegedly largely environmental. To fulfill commitments made in the Kyoto Protocol, the region must address emissions coming from the transport sector.[17] The heavy irony is that as the policy makers in the EU push for cleaner fuel burn and lowered greenhouse-gas emissions, their palm oil imports from Malaysia, Indonesia, and Brazil actually destroy rainforests; threaten biodiversity; cause the conversion of tropical peatlands, which creates carbon emissions; and may even lead to the extinction of the orangutan.[18]

Aside from the glaring environmental problems, the agrofuels program also comes with great social costs. The Transnational Institute reports that the activities of an oil palm plantation in Cameroon resulted in land confiscation, bad labor practices, and pollution.[19]

Jutta Kill offers a good analysis of the fragile assumptions of the EU agrofuels policy:

> Investment in well-designed and affordable public transport schemes is essential, but the EU blueprint makes no mention of these. The paper leaves no doubt that "energy security," not climate change or reducing the EU's environmental footprint, is the primary objective of increasing biofuel use in Europe's transport sector. That may explain the lack of attention to measures within the transport sector that could bring about much greater climate change gains. Speed limits and a better power-to-weight ratio for new cars and trucks could result in the same savings; and even greater savings could be achieved by adopting fuel-efficient tyres and reducing fuel consumption through smaller engines in passenger cars. And this all before we get into fuel savings from substituting individualised transport systems through smart public transport schemes. The Commission discards all these options as marginal and not worth pursuing. It prefers risky biofuel imports that are likely to undermine climate and environmental policies over climate-proofing the EU's transport sector. No wonder, then, that over sixty environmental and social justice organisations are already calling for a halt on EU biofuel targets.[20]

Brazil: Agrofuel Superpower

Brazil has been producing agrofuels for the past thirty years. Ethanol made from sugarcane accounts for most of its agrofuel production. The South American country is the second largest ethanol producer after the United States and the largest exporter.

In April 2008, President Luiz ("Lula") Inácio da Silva vehemently denied that Brazilian sugarcane-based ethanol was contributing to the food price crisis and criticized a UN report advising strong caution in pursuing agrofuels production incentives. While studies such as the Mitchell report absolve Brazilian ethanol of significant impacts on food prices, it cannot be absolved of negative environmental and social impacts. Brazilian agrofuels are said to have caused deforestation in the Amazon, losses in biodiversity, and bad, even slavelike working conditions.

Ethanol made from sugarcane may be more energy-efficient than corn-based ethanol, but it is incredibly labor-inefficient to produce.[21] The Brazil Renewable Energy Company makes up for this inefficiency by "paying workers less than a dollar an hour, packing them cheek-to-jowl in substandard living conditions, preventing them from leaving the unsanitary housing on their free time, feeding them poorly, and (rather ironically for an ethanol manufacturer) banning alcohol."[22] In November 2008, the Catholic Church's *Pastoral da Terra* commission in Brazil reported that almost seven thousand workers living in slave-like conditions have been freed since 2003.[23]

While the Brazilian government attacks the US ethanol subsidies, it is quiet about the fact that Brazilian agribusiness will also benefit hugely, though indirectly, from those measures. With more and more US land diverted to produce agrofuel feedstock, Brazil will rush into the vacuum, especially in soybean production.[24] This land will come from coastal forests, the *cerrado* or savanna and even the Amazon, where wildlife and forests will be threatened. Sabrina Valle of the *Washington Post* reported on the certainty of environmental degradation:

The agriculture business and the Brazilian government say that there are nearly 350,000 square miles of already-cleared land available for agricultural expansion in the Cerrado. The government says more than 115,000 square miles of cattle pastures could be used—that's enough land to more than double soybean production and increase sugarcane production five times and ethanol by at least 10.

"Brazil is the only country with a vast amount of land available for immediate expansion of sustainable agriculture. If the US races after ethanol, soybean prices tend to climb and demand will be supplied by Brazil," said Carlo Lovatelli, corporate affairs director for Bunge, one of the largest soy traders in Brazil, headquartered in White Plains, N.Y.

Lovatelli, who also represents companies responsible for 93 percent of all soy traded in Brazil, said that if demand escalates, Brazilian production could double in as little as three to four years. And the target region has already been chosen: "Cerrado is perfect for agriculture and will be used— there is no question about it," Lovatelli said.[25]

In sum, US and European Union agrofuels policies have triggered a dangerous chain reaction in the South. Developing countries now rush in to fill the demand for agrofuels as US and EU policies set targets that their own agricultural systems cannot fill. Governments and business groups in Latin America and Southeast Asia scramble to fill this demand at the expense of workers' rights and the environment. Land use changes in the United States, in addition, spell a bonanza for Southern agribusiness groups: soybean production expands in countries like Brazil as the United States takes land away from soybeans to devote to subsidized ethanol. The ultimate victim: the environment, as Brazil and other countries respond to the demand by vigorously hacking away their forests.[26]

The Contours of the Global Agrofuels Regime

Countries in the North and South alike are being seduced by the promise of agrofuels: a measure of energy security and independence from Middle Eastern oil. The gyrations in the price of crude in the world market and the fragile security situation in many regions provide a strong lure and impetus for countries to pursue alternative hard-energy sources. Moreover, the idea of putting corn and oilseeds in the gas tank appears to be a plus for the environment. The countryside seems to ensure a comparatively stable source of renewable energy.

Everybody seems to be jumping onto the bandwagon, from the United States and the EU to China, the Philippines, Brazil, and South Africa, to name a few. Agrofuels promise rural development, lower greenhouse gas emissions, and a potentially unlimited supply of fuel—any country that can produce sugarcane, beets, corn, or wheat can make their own fuel. It is no wonder that in the past decade there has been a proliferation of laws, mandates, and other mechanisms to encourage agrofuels production across different regions and countries.

Regional organizations actively promote cooperation and technology transfer in this area. In January 2007, members of the Association of Southeast Asian Nations (ASEAN) signed the Cebu Declaration on East Asian Energy Security, which encouraged even the oil exporting country Brunei to jump onto the agrofuels bandwagon. The declaration encouraged the pursuit of alternative energy sources and expressed broad support for cooperation in the development of agrofuels in the region.[27] The Asia-Pacific Economic Cooperation (APEC) organization is also actively supporting agrofuels production and consumption among its member countries, principally through the APEC Biofuels Task Force that has been meeting regularly since 2006. Newcomers in the field include Australia, with four ethanol plants in operation in November 2007, and Vietnam, whose government approved an agrofuels plan to develop ethanol and biodiesel.[28] More and more countries in the region are encouraged to diversify their energy portfolio in this direction. In Latin America the United Nations Economic Commission for Latin America and the Caribbean (ECLAC) seeks a common approach to agrofuels development and serves as a forum on issues related to it. ECLAC and other organizations endorsed sugar-based ethanol in a book published in November 2008.[29] Widely hailed in the region as a success story, Brazilian ethanol is being hyped as a model for agrofuels production in the region. The African Union also sponsored a high-level seminar on agrofuels in 2007 that led to the adoption of the Addis Ababa Declaration on Sustainable Biofuels Development in Africa. This trumpets a ten-year agrofuels development program that includes ethanol, biomass, and biodiesel production.[30]

The agrofuels boom resembles the emergence of a financial bubble. It is all too easy to join the bandwagon. For governments and consumers alike, agrofuels are the easy choice. Middle-class consumers can continue to use their cars as much as they like. Governments do not need to rethink and re-engineer transport systems and policies. Consumption patterns do not need to be re-evaluated. The environment will benefit and local development will be spurred in the developing world. Everybody will be happy.

Well, some will, and most won't; for among the realities accompanying this pleasant dream are the huge land-lease deals taking place in land-rich countries like the Philippines, Cambodia, and Madagascar.[31] There are widespread reports in international media of private firms and governments from countries that lack arable land striking lease agreements. Some of these deals are for food production, others for agrofuels, but with agriculture being commodified, what is produced on the leased lands will ultimately depend on what is most profitable to bring to the global market at a given time.

The most notable of these deals is the Korean firm Daewoo Logistics' plan to buy a ninety-nine-year lease on more than three million acres of land in Madagascar for agrofuels production. Maize and palm oil will be cultivated on almost half the arable land in the country.[32]

Similarly, Cambodia and the Philippines are negotiating "agricultural investment" projects. Kuwait is trading loans for Cambodian produce. The Philippines and Qatar are currently negotiating the lease of 100,000 hectares of land.[33] In effect, the food crisis and energy crisis are causing countries to secure food supplies and agrofuel feedstock in unconventional ways. It is no longer sufficient to import grains. The land that produces that grain must be secured through contracts. Land is now the desired commodity, to the detriment of local populations who depend on the land for their own food consumption. Political elites in land-rich countries appear to be all too happy to oblige at the expense of their own country's food security. One thing is sure: the ranks of the hungry and the landless will increase, and so will the pressures on the environment.

The World Bank is often on the wrong side of things, but in the case of agrofuels, it is on the right side. Its prediction for the Philippines may well apply to other countries:

> The expected increase in demand for sugar for ethanol production, abetted by the incentives provided by the Biofuel Act which, among others, mandates a minimum amount of bio-fuel use, can be expected to further pull sugar prices up, and consequently food prices. In addition, the bio-fuel policy will most likely put pressure on extending cultivation on marginal lands and converting forests to agricultural uses, thereby worsening the impact of agriculture on natural resources. Finally, it is also expected that this policy will increase both the value of sugarcane farms and the difficulty in completing the Comprehensive Agrarian Reform Program in these areas.[34]

The Ultimate Technofix

More than energy security, agrofuels promise clean energy. Compared with fossil fuels, ethanol and biodiesel are supposed to have a cleaner burn and are supposedly carbon neutral. Agrofuels are, along with nuclear power and carbon capture and storage technology (CCST), one of the technofixes that the global economic and political establishment have endorsed as solutions to global warming. In fact they are "solutions" that allow societies to defer pursuing the only effective approach to the climate crisis, which is to radically reduce consumption, especially in the North. Agrofuels, nuclear power, CCST—all encourage the illusion that Western-style economic growth can continue without causing environmental destabilization provided everyone shifts to nonfossil fuels—an easy solution to the climate crisis.

This message—that growth can continue as before with more benign energy sources—comes straight from multilateral institutions that promote agrofuels. In the background studies supporting the initiatives of the Asian Development Bank (ADB) to promote the bioenergy programs in the Greater Mekong Subregion, the ADB stresses that the lack of access to energy services is one of the bottlenecks toward achieving high levels of economic growth.[35] The common solution offered to the problem of increasing energy demands without exacerbating the climate crisis is to "diversify" sources of energy.

The consortium of UN agencies working for energy security, UN-Energy, in a paper sponsored by no less than the Food and Agriculture Organization, talks about pursuing an "optimal energy mix" that decision makers will have to carefully choose in order to meet energy needs and protect the environment.[36] This implies that in order to support the ever-increasing rate of energy consumption justified by the pursuit of growth, developing countries must look to new frontiers of energy sources. Both institutions refuse to acknowledge that the high levels of energy consumption are the problem in the first place and that bringing them down is what institutions should be concerned about. That, however, strikes at the very heart of capitalism, the survival of which depends on constantly rising consumption and constantly expanding production.

There is no easy solution to climate change. Nuclear power is simply dangerous. CCST is science fiction at this stage. And the trade-off between the expansion of agrofuel production and the exacerbation of the food crisis and the displacement of small farmers is simply too high a price.

The Future of Agrofuels

In response to the food crisis and the incontrovertible role that agrofuel production played in exacerbating it, the OECD (also known as the "club of rich countries") has called for a moratorium on expanding agrofuels production and for a reduction in the overall consumption of fuels for automobiles.[37] According to the organization's findings, policies promoting cutbacks in energy consumption will benefit the environment better than pursuing an agrofuels policy. The report argues that focus should be put on reducing energy consumption:

> This is especially important in the transport sector where the growth in energy use and related environmental problems is more pronounced. In particular, this includes the gradual move from highly energy intensive modes of transport to less intensive ones, and improvement in fuel efficiency in all transport sectors. Generally the costs of reducing GHG [greenhouse gas] emissions by saving energy are lower than by switching to alternative energy sources, in particular biofuels.[38]

Environmental and social justice groups and other actors are calling for cutbacks on targets and subsidies, and in some cases even the total abolition of the programs. As they stand, production targets have greatly compromised development in poor countries, where households typically spend about half their income on food. Oxfam calculates that the agrofuels programs of the US and EU have pushed 30 million people below the poverty line. ActionAid estimates that $16 billion to $18 billion every year is being spent on subsidies to US and EU farmers—more than four times the total agricultural aid to the South. This policy is putting about 260 million people at risk of hunger, according to the group. Concerns have been raised that agrofuels programs in the US and EU may severely compromise the steps taken to reach the millennium development goals (MDGs) and that they may have caused reversals of recent achievements in poverty reduction in developing countries.

The debate over agrofuels has resulted in different responses from the EU and the United States. In July 2008, the United Kingdom's Renewable Fuels Agency came out with the Gallagher report that recommends the lowering of the country's agrofuels target from 10 percent of energy by 2020 to 5 percent by 2013–14.[39] The findings of the report recognized that agrofuels have a negative impact on food security and the environment and that these effects should be studied more carefully before ambitious targets are aggressively pursued. However, the report also stressed the "immense" potential of agrofuels in lowering greenhouse gas emissions as long as strict environmental standards are in place. Although the report called for lower targets, it rejected a moratorium on agrofuels production such as that being proposed by the OECD. A moratorium "will reduce the ability of the agrofuels industry to invest in new technologies . . . [and] will make it significantly more difficult for the potential of agrofuels to be realised."[40] The British government is beginning to recognize the realities of agrofuel production, but hasn't as yet undertaken more-effective alternative energy programs. Moreover, how the government plans to implement the target cutbacks remains to be seen as policies at the EU level are apparently unchanging.

Thus far, the solutions being proffered and considered include stricter controls on land-use change, the exploration of second-generation agrofuels that are said not to compete with food production, technological advances in electric cars, and a reevaluation of the set targets. The report remained optimistic on the sustainability of the agrofuels industry provided that strong policies, benchmarks, and indicators on land-use change and deforestation are put in place not only in the European region, but also in South America, Southeast Asia, and Africa, where the EU imports agrofuels. This agenda was brought to the attention of other developed countries at the G8 summit in Japan in July 2008.

The EU, Slovenia, France, the UK, Germany, and Italy are all echoing concerns over the negative impacts of agrofuels on the environment and food prices, and policy makers are welcoming a rethinking of the agreed-upon regional targets.[41] As of this writing, the European Parliament was still debating the sustainability criteria, particularly on indirect land use for agrofuel production and importation.[42] The EU is not expected to provide a set of sustainability criteria until the end of 2010.

But the formulation and implementation of sustainability criteria, however foolproof, would not address the main problems in the agrofuels market. First, the set of criteria would have to be universally accepted in order to have any significant effect. If, for example, the EU implements the criteria and the United States does not, the situation would favor the United States, which can continue importing palm oil and ethanol from the South, refine the oil and ethanol with large subsidies, and export the commodities abroad. But, more important, instituting these standards is a poor substitute for addressing the real problem of overconsumption. As Gretchen Gordon writes,

Policy makers are looking for ways to use regulatory creativity to distinguish between "good" and "bad" biofuels. However, the basic framework for a global free market in biofuels remains unquestioned and the push to turn biofuels into global commodities is proceeding apace.

Those seeking to regulate biofuels must bear three important points in mind: (1) The current biofuels trade model is one of industrial export agriculture that brings with it negative environmental and social impacts; (2) efforts to mitigate these impacts through narrow regulation of biofuels without addressing the dynamics of agriculture, energy and financial markets will be ineffective; and (3) the free market in industrial biofuels threatens to detract from real solutions to the energy crisis and equitable development needs.[43]

While the EU at least has been reconsidering its agrofuels program, the same cannot be said of the United States. In April 2008, Texas governor Rick Perry filed a request to the EPA to waive the renewable fuel standard by 50 percent, saying that high feedstock prices were harming the livestock industry. The EPA denied this request. Observers claim that there is no reason to believe that the United States will change its mind about the agrofuels targets it has set.[44] Policy directions under the new leadership in the White House remain uncertain, as Barack Obama may well be torn between supporting the agrofuels program as he has done in the past and taking serious steps to help manage the food price crisis, which agrofuel production exacerbated. It is worth noting that Obama's home state of Illinois is the second largest corn-producing state in the United States.

With energy demand dropping amid the global economic crisis and the price of oil collapsing, agrofuel production may become less and less profitable. It is not likely to be phased out anytime soon, however, since there are too many interests that have a stake in its development and too many myths that sustain it as a solution to global warming.

Conclusion

Too many false claims have been made about agrofuels: that they are renewable and therefore sustainable, that they will bring development in the South, that they do not impact food prices, and that they provide the way forward through the efficient use and development of technology to combat climate change. Eric Holt-Gimenez of Food First explains the source of the continuing myths about agrofuels:

> in reality, biofuel draws its power from cornucopian myths and directs our attention away from economic interests that would benefit from the transition, while avoiding discussion of the growing North–South food and energy imbalance.
>
> They obscure the political-economic relationships between land, people, resources and food, and fail to help us understand the profound consequences of the industrial transformation of our food and fuel systems.[15]

But the myths rest on a structure of interlocking interests. Big corporations see biofuels as an eventual source of great profit. International and regional organizations and governments are only too happy to endorse agrofuels as a solution because it strikes them as a politically viable one through which apparently everybody wins   corporate agricultural interests, small farmers, politicians, and the environment.

Yet, over the past few years, developments have taken the sheen off the agrofuel promise. Reports of negative environmental impacts abound, from pollution to the clearing away of forests, peatlands, and carbon sinks to threats to biodiversity. There are even reports claiming that corn ethanol and biodiesel production processes consume vast amounts of fossil fuels, defeating the whole purpose of developing agrofuels.[46] The veiled reality is that corporate agriculture and political elites may be the only beneficiaries. The promise of development to small communities has not materialized. Instead we have stories of human rights abuse and slavelike labor practices, conflicts between leasing land to foreign investors and agrarian reform, displacement of small-scale farmers, a misappropriation of land-for-food to land-for-fuel, and hunger even in traditionally food-secure countries.

If there is anything that has become clear to large numbers of people, it is that agrofuels are not a benign alternative to fossil fuels.

Chapter 7

Resistance and the Road to the Future

September 10, 2003, the opening day of the fifth ministerial meeting of the World Trade Organization in Cancún, Mexico, was also a day of street protest against the World Trade Organization. Within the halls of the Cancún Convention Center, negotiations in agricultural trade were polarizing, with the newly formed Group of 20 and Group of 33, two coalitions of developing countries, refusing to make any more concessions to the United States and European Union, which were determined to preserve their massive subsidies for the large farming interests while demanding greater market access to developing country markets. A flurry of activity broke out in the ranks of the demonstrators facing the police barricades, and I saw someone being hauled away. I assumed he had been hurt in a scuffle with the police. Only about an hour later did I learn that the Korean farmer Lee Kyung Hae had taken his own life in protest against the WTO.

Lee was one of the exceptional figures and organizations that have made the new peasant movement, in the eyes of many in global civil society, the epitome of dedication, courage, imagination, innovative organizing, and élan over the last decade, taking up the role that the industrial working class filled decades ago. Suddenly, farmers and peasants were taking the lead in national and international mobilizations against globalization, neoliberalism, and capitalism. Unfailingly, in every big protest against the World Trade Organization, the bête noire of the global movement for economic justice, farmers groups would be on the front lines, just as Lee was, on top of a steel barricade, that fateful day.

Movement Profile I: Lee Kyung Hae

In the days after his suicide, Lee, a model farmer who lost his farm owing to trade liberalization, became the symbol of the plight of the world's small farmers and peasants and of the global opposition to the WTO. Shocked, the delegates at the convention center observed a moment of silence to mark his passing. When the ministerial meeting collapsed in disarray two days later, the thousands of protesters who had come to Cancún were certain that Lee's suicide had contributed to the debacle. If ever there was a death that was not in vain, this was it.

For non-Koreans, Lee's suicide was astonishing. In Korean civil society, however, altruistic suicide, to borrow the term of the sociologist Émile Durkheim, is an honorable tradition. One of the birth pangs of the modern Korean labor movement was the self-immolation, in November 1970, of Jeon Tae-Il, a leading organizer of young women workers in the garment district of Seoul. "Suicide," Jeon's brother told me when I was doing research in Korea in the late '80s, "is the expression of passion for the people, of the purest love."[1] This spirit was carried over to the student movement of the 1980s, where altruistic suicide by idealistic student activists became one of the weapons of the movement for democratization of the political system.

The man who brought altruistic suicide to the international activist scene was a member of the Korea Peasants' League, a coalition of peasant networks that was founded in 1990. While its founding was mainly motivated by opposition to trade liberalization, the KPL traced farmers' plight to the second-class status to which agriculture had been relegated in Korea's economy. In its founding declaration, the organization blamed the Korean dictator Park Chung Hee's "policy of development focused on industrialization that was based on sacrifice of farmers."[2] The KPL served as the flying wedge of the protests and street battles that swirled in the streets of Hong Kong on the occasion of the next ministerial meeting of the WTO, in December 2005. Admired for its discipline and for street tactics honed in years of battles with the Korean police, the KPL led the charge that nearly succeeded in breaking police lines at the Hong Kong Convention Center on December 17. KPL activists made up a significant part of the more than nine hundred people who were subsequently arrested by police.

Movement Profile II: José Bové

Prominent among the protesters in Hong Kong was José Bové, the iconic French farmer who was one of the founders of the now forty-thousand-strong Confédération Paysanne. Perhaps more than any other figure, Bové changed the image of the Northern farmer from a faceless subsidized entity to that of "a small man from Massif Central," as French newspapers described him, who was engaged in a David-versus-Goliath struggle against the global agribusiness complex and genetic engineering. He led the much publicized dismantling of a McDonald's outlet that was about to open in his hometown of Millau, France, on August 12, 1999— an act for which he was sent to prison—and contributed to forging an enduring link between the rising international farmers' movement and the antiglobalization movement, the alternative agriculture movement, and the environmental movement. In an interview with the *New Left Review* in which he recounted the action, Bové showed a keen sensitivity to how the farmers' movement could crystallize not only the interests of farmers but those of a much broader, varied constituency that had become disillusioned with corporate-driven globalization:

When we said we would protest by dismantling the half-built McDonald's in our town, everyone understood why—the symbolism was so strong. It was for proper food against *malbouffe* [junk food], agricultural workers against multinationals. The actual structure was incredibly flimsy. We piled the door-frames and partitions on to our tractor trailers and drove them through the town. The extreme Right and other nationalists tried to make out it was anti-Americanism, but the vast majority understood it was no such thing. It was a protest against a form of food production that wants to dominate the world.[3]

Bové has had his share of detractors, including people who ridicule his claim of being a sheep farmer or accuse him of grandstanding. But no one questions his determination to bring the plight of the world's peasants to the center of world attention.

Movement Profile III: João Pedro Stédile and the MST

Bové is one of the leading lights of Via Campesina, the international farmers' federation. So is João Pedro Stédile, one of the founding members of the MST or *Movimento dos Trabalhadores Rurais Sem Terra* (Landless Workers' Movement). Stédile made international headlines when he excluded President Luis ("Lula") Inácio da Silva from a meeting between civil society activists and South American presidents at the January 2009 World Social Forum in Belém, Brazil, allegedly to punish Lula for his weak support for progressive reform and his backing of Brazilian agribusiness. But the four presidents who attended—Venezuela's Hugo Chávez, Bolivia's Evo Morales, Ecuador's Rafael Correa, and Paraguay's Fernando Lugo—did not have it easy either; they were subjected to friendly fire by Stédile, who said, "You have had some achievements but you have to do more in your countries to make a real difference."

MST is probably the most dynamic agrarian mass movement in any country in the world today. It has been able to combine solid gains on the ground for its members with a radical strategic thrust. Brazilian government agencies defy it at their peril, as the PT (Workers' Party) government of Lula has learned. Their ability to innovatively operate at the local, national, and international levels has been nothing short of dazzling and marks MST as the paradigmatic globalized social movement. From its meticulously planned land occupations to its highly publicized destruction of fields planted with Monsanto-engineered GM seeds, MST has combined professionalism, radicalism, and imagination.

In an effort to try to explain the success of MST compared with the Landless People's Movement in South Africa, a recent analysis brings up three factors that played a key role in the MST case: a dedicated leadership of politicized activists who were themselves "sons and daughters of small farmers"; a core strategy of land occupation which "provide[s] the space of movement production and reproduction," where members "realize what the movement is really about"; and the movement's determined stance of preserving its autonomy from political parties.[4]

One might add here that MST developed an underlying perspective or stance that responds to the fundamental thrust of contemporary global capitalism. In his interview with *New Left Review,* Stédile describes this dynamic in comparison with the Zapatista (EZLN) movement in Mexico:

[The Zapatistas'] is, at root, a struggle of indigenous peoples for autonomy—and if there's a criticism to be made of their experience, it would be that the slowness of their advance is due to their inability to broaden it into a class struggle, a national one. They have accepted the terms of fighting for a specific ethnicity within a particular territory—whereas ours is a farmers' movement that has been transformed and politicized as a result of the advance of capitalism, of neoliberalism.[5]

This broadening of MST's perspective had a number of implications for its future trajectory. One is that the MST struggle had to go beyond "just . . . a movement for agrarian reform, seeking only to meet the needs of its own sector."[6] It had to be part of a broader coalition of forces that were in a transformative struggle against neoliberal globalization. At this particular global turning point, MST also felt it was no longer sufficient to argue that the land belongs to those who work it; instead, "[W]e want an agrarian practice that transforms farmers into guardians of the land, and a different way of farming, that ensures an ecological equilibrium and also guarantees that land is not seen as private property."[7] The time was ripe: "The realities of neoliberal internationalization" have "created the conditions for farmers to unite against the neoliberal model," and necessitated an internationalist political response.[8] Not surprisingly, MST has been one of the central actors in Via Campesina, an international coalition that represents, from Stédile's view, "the very striking" development that finally "farmers are starting to achieve a degree of worldwide coordination, after five hundred years of capitalist development."[9]

MST members, however, are the first to deflate any one-sided, romantic view of their movement. It has made its share of mistakes, including, as Raj Patel points out, a disastrous experiment with trying to enforce cooperatives as the main mode of farm production in the 1980s. It is, however, the leadership and membership's commitment to the democratic process in resolving differences, no matter how messy, that has seen the organization through. Today, it has "robust mechanisms of direct and representative democracy."[10]

While Stédile frankly admits that "the MST as an organized force of the workers of Brazil is very small,"[11] the organization has had an impact beyond its numbers. It has been able to pressure the government to settle more than 370,000 families on land, a figure that translates into millions of people.[12] Under the slogan "Each and every landless person studying," it has advanced popular education and contributed to increasing adult literacy, working with federal and state universities as well as with foreign governments such as Venezuela and Cuba.[13] But beyond its measurable achievements, indeed, beyond its symbols, strategy, tactical skills, and admired leadership, what makes MST so attractive, Monica Dias Martins contends, is the way its current practices might prefigure the future:

> In addition to the impressive strategy of the *festa* (land occupation), four vital concepts seem to arise from MST practice: a collective way of life that ranges across the spectrum of activities from basic food production to the artistic process, the work-and-study educational method, an expressed respect for a diversity of opinions with a unity of perspectives, and an insistent confrontation with the neoliberal project.
>
> The MST practice is being closely observed by the landless themselves and by Brazilian society in general, not as a laboratory experiment in free market policy . . . but as the embryo of a new society that can come to life through the combined efforts of the various popular sectors. The MST appears to have the capacity to transform the collective dream of the millions of Brazilians who want a better life into radical actions and perspectives. It remains to be seen whether it will do so.[14]

Via Campesina and the Peasant Way

Via Campesina, to which MST, José Bové, and Lee Kyung Hae belonged, has become the face of the peasant internationalism that has captured the imagination of global civil society. Making its formal debut in 1993, Via has grown to an international network of more than 150 national and subnational organizations from fifty-six countries. Its ranks include other impressive peasant leaders, such as Nettie Wiebe of Canada, Rafael Alegria of Honduras, Henry Saragih of Indonesia, and Paul Nicholson of the Basque Country. In just over fifteen years, Via Campesina has catapulted into the front ranks of global civil society. Its green detachments were important actors in Seattle in December 1999, in the massive demonstrations against the Group of Eight in Genoa in June 2001, and in the anti-WTO actions in Cancún in September 2003 and in Hong Kong in December 2005. One of its central achievements has been helping to unravel the Doha Round of trade negotiations of the WTO.

Via has several key features that mark it as a unique actor in global civil society.

First of all is its leadership, most of whom are farmer-activists. Direct leadership by members of the class being represented is not common in many political parties, unions, and mass movements, where it is often middle-class intellectuals or activists who provide both political and intellectual leadership. In the process of its emergence, Via had to break with NGOs that sought to provide leadership to the peasant movement and to confine it to "policy research"; Via's "difficult birth" saw farmer-activists struggle to take the reins of the organization, with a vision and strategy for directly confronting neoliberal globalization.[15]

Second, Via has combined a radical vision, a capacity for coalition building, a repertoire of tactics ranging from lobbying to direct action, and professional handling of the media to become a force to be reckoned with. A key reason for Via's success is the priority it puts on gaining allies and helping to build broad networks. This is not simply a matter of ground-war tactics but of an overall strategy—one with a fundamental premise. This premise is that, as Paul Nicholson, a member of the International Coordinating Committee, puts it, "[a]cross our organizations, in the South as well as in the North, there is a clear sense that we have to change the society if we want to change the agricultural policies. We cannot defend farmers' interests without challenging the neo-liberal system as a whole. Small farmers will not get land if the whole structure of society is not transformed."[16] One consequence of the effective deployment of its varied skills is that, though Via represents marginalized masses, it does not have a marginal voice. One measure of its broad credibility is the fact that in 2008, the London *Guardian* named the Indonesian peasant leader Henry Saragih, Via Campesina's current coordinator, as one of its "ultimate green heroes," among the "50 people who could save the planet."[17]

Third, largely owing to the determination of its outspoken women activists, Via has, perhaps more than any other large progressive international group, successfully put gender at the front and center of its agenda, though this process was not without conflicts and frustrations. Indeed, Via has been regarded as a "good example" to other movements for its establishment of parity of representation between men and women in the organization's most powerful body, the International Coordinating Committee.[18]

Fourth, Via has, again probably better than many other movement organizations, managed to bridge the North–South divide among its member organizations by constantly stressing the common farmer and peasant roots of its rank and file, consistently promoting the perspective that neoliberalism has destroyed livelihoods both in the South and the North, and elaborating organizational mechanisms that promote inclusiveness as well as regional parity.[19]

But like all movements, Via has had its share of problems. One of these, the prominent agrarian specialist Saturnino Borras Jr. points out, have been the tensions between a bloc of small farmers and the landless in its ranks. Land reform has been a central advocacy of Via, yet one of its most influential members, the Karnataka State Farmers' Association (KRRS) of India, which has a base mainly of middle and rich farmers, opposed making land reform a major campaign. KRRS played a very important role in the global, regional, and national campaigns against GMOs and American fast food, being responsible for dismantling the Kentucky Fried Chicken outlet in Bangalore, the state capital.[20] But Via's effectiveness in South Asia has apparently been negatively affected by KRRS's class-determined stances. "In the case of KRRS," notes Borras, "a significant proportion of the organized section of the rural-based exploited social classes not only in India but in South Asia more generally were excluded from the Via Campesina process, either because KRRS blocked their entry into Via Campesina or they refused to participate in the process where the 'gatekeeper' was KRRS."[21] Yet to Via's credit, land reform was adopted as a central campaign despite KRRS's opposition, and a number of organizations of poor and landless farmers in South Asia were eventually brought into the organization. And to its credit, KRRS remains in Via, accepting the principles of pluralism and diversity of membership that are among the pillars of the coalition.

Via has a well elaborated, radical critique of the current agrifood paradigm. It questions all the basic premises of this paradigm—monoculture, large-scale industrial farming, the Green Revolution, and biotechnology—and shows that far from being an effective producer of food, the paradigm subordinates food production to the logic of profit, promotes dislocation and dispossession of millions, and tailors agricultural production to the needs of those with market power, thus creating the very hunger it is supposed to banish. Moreover, contrary to its claims of efficiency, the costs of industrial agriculture, in terms of chemical pollution, soil and genetic erosion, carbon emissions, and tremendous subsidies for agribusiness, outweigh the benefits.

While it sees its struggle against this system as unfolding on many fronts, Via Campesina claims neutralizing the WTO as the sine qua non of its other initiatives, since the WTO is the linchpin of the neoliberal order, establishing the rules and conventions that underpin the creation and maintenance of the global free market. Thus Via's key campaign has been to derail the agriculture negotiations of the WTO Doha Round, an objective it has pursued with an impressive array of tactics ranging from mass demonstrations to lobbying negotiators in Geneva.

Yet even as it has engaged in resistance, Via has put equal weight on trying to articulate an alternative to the current agrifood order. This alternative does not only consist of land reform, the traditional peasant demand, but showcases a program called "food sovereignty." As Annette Desmarais notes, Via Campesina, along with several allies, elaborated the concept in opposition to reformist efforts to ensure the right to food within the WTO paradigm by introducing (among other things) a "development box" that would spell out exceptions to trade liberalization. Following their introduction of the concept of food sovereignty at an international meeting in 1996, the organization spent several years filling out, nuancing, and popularizing the proposal:

> Peasant and farm organizations clearly understood that nothing less than radical transformation was needed to stop the ongoing displacement, marginalization, repression, and persistent impoverishment of rural peoples. Reforming or "fixing" existing structures would do little to stop the increasing levels of hunger, depopulation, and environmental devastation in rural areas. By introducing food sovereignty, the Via Campesina was clearly challenging everyone concerned to think outside the boxes—technological fixes, liberalization, deregulation, and privatization—that often characterize policy deliberations about food and agriculture.[22]

Food Sovereignty

What are the elements of the food sovereignty paradigm? A number of themes have emerged from the writings of Via, its leaders, intellectuals with roots in farming such as Annette

Desmarais, Via's allies, and the broader coalitions within which it participates.

First, the goal of agricultural policy should be food self-sufficiency. A country's farmers should produce most of the food consumed domestically—a condition not covered by the concept of "food security" that US corporate representatives have defined as the capacity to fill a country's food needs through either domestic production or imports. As noted earlier, the former US agriculture secretary John Block redefined food security in this manner: "[T]he idea that developing countries should feed themselves is an anachronism from a bygone era. They could better ensure their food security by relying on US agricultural products, which are available, in most cases at lower cost."[23]

Second, a people should have the right to determine their patterns of food production and consumption, taking into consideration "rural and productive diversity," and not allow these to be subordinated to unregulated international trade.[24]

Third, production and consumption of food should be guided by the welfare of farmers and consumers, not the profit projections of transnational agribusiness.

Fourth, national food systems must produce "healthy, good quality, and culturally appropriate food primarily for the domestic market,"[25] and avoid what Bové has called *malbouffe* or internationally standardized or "junk food."[26]

Fifth, a new balance must be achieved between agriculture and industry, the countryside and the city, to reverse the subordination of agriculture and the countryside to industry and urban elites, which has resulted in a blighted countryside and massive urban slums of rural refugees.

Sixth, the consolidation of land by landlords and transnational firms must be reversed and equity in land distribution must be promoted through land reform. Reform should also include provisions for communal and collective forms of ownership and production that promote a sense of ecological stewardship.

Seventh, agricultural production should be carried out mainly by small farmers or cooperative or state enterprises, and the distribution and consumption of food should be governed by fair pricing schemes that take into consideration the rights and welfare of both farmers and consumers. Among other things, this means an end to dumping by transnational firms of subsidized agricultural commodities, which has artificially brought down prices, resulting in the destruction of small farmers. It would also mean, according to the activist-scholar Peter Rosset, "a return to protection of the national food production of nations . . . rebuilding national grain reserves . . . public sector budgets, floor prices, credit and other forms of support" that "stimulate the recovery of [countries'] food production capacity."[27]

Eighth, industrial agriculture based on genetic engineering and the original chemical-intensive Green Revolution should be discouraged, because monopoly control over seeds advances the corporate agenda and because industrial agriculture is environmentally unsustainable.

Ninth, traditional peasant and indigenous agricultural technologies contain a great deal of wisdom and represent the evolution of a largely benign balance between the human community and the biosphere. Thus the evolution of agrotechnology to meet social needs must take traditional practices as a starting point rather than overthrowing them as obsolete.

Valorizing Peasant Knowledge

The food sovereignty perspective valorizes elements—peasant agriculture, small-scale production, the environment—that have been devalued by capitalism and simply considered as barriers to progressive modes of economic organization. The characteristics of peasant agriculture—the closeness to the land, the organic tie between family and farm, the focus on the local market, the labor-intensity of production, the sense of working with rather than dominating nature—are elements that have evolved to respond to the needs of ecological stability, community, and governance, and are not to be thrown away in the cavalier way that industrial capitalist agriculture has done.

This valorization is not a defensive mechanism meant to postpone the passing of a doomed mode of production, but looks to the future, as one of the elements of a larger process of transformation. As Philip McMichael puts it, "food sovereignty in theory and practice represents a political, ecological, and cultural alternative to a 'high modernist' corporate agriculture premised on standardized inputs and outputs and serving a minority of the world's population . . . the principle of food sovereignty embodies neither a return to traditional agriculture, nor a return to a bucolic peasant culture—rather, it is a thoroughly modern response to the current neoliberal conjuncture, which has no sustainable solutions to its thoroughly modern problems."[28]

Desmarais echoes this idea that food sovereignty is not a statement of anti-modernity but an espousal of an alternative modernity:

> The peasant model advocated by the Via Campesina does not entail a rejection of modernity, or of technology and trade, accompanied by a romanticized return to an archaic past steeped in rustic traditions. Rather, the Via Campesina insists that an alternative model must be based on certain ethics and values in which culture and social justice count for something and concrete mechanisms are put in place to ensure a future without hunger. The Via Campesina's alternative model entails recapturing aspects of traditional, local, or farmers' knowledge, and combining that knowledge with new technology when and where it is appropriate to do so.[29]

She points out that "[b]y integrating careful borrowings with traditional practice, peasants and small-scale farmers everywhere are reaffirming the lessons from their histories and reshaping the rural landscape to benefit those who work the land as they collectively redefine what food is produced, how it is produced, and where and for whom."[30]

The Technology Question

It is well and good to affirm the benign character of peasant agriculture, but does it really respond to the great demands on agriculture in our time? As noted earlier, even scholars sympathetic to the plight of the peasantry or rural workers such as Henry Bernstein claim that advocacy of the peasant way "largely ignores issues of feeding the world's population, which has grown so greatly almost everywhere in the modern epoch, in significant part because of the revolution in productivity achieved by the development of capitalism."[31]

Advocates of the peasant way respond, first of all, that the superiority in terms of production of industrial capitalist agriculture is not sustained empirically. Miguel Altieri and Clara Nicholls, for instance, point out that although conventional wisdom is that small farms are backward and unproductive, in fact, "research shows that small farms are much more productive than large farms if total output is considered rather than yield from a single crop. Small integrated farming systems that produce grains, fruits, vegetables, fodder, and animal products outproduce yield per unit of single crops such as corn (monocultures) on large-scale farms."[32] Moreover, when one factors in the ecological destabilization that has accompanied the generalization of industrial agriculture, the balance of costs and benefits lurches sharply toward the negative. For instance, Daniel Imhoff has noted that in the United States,

> the average food item journeys some 1,300 miles before becoming part of a meal. Fruits and vegetables are refrigerated, waxed, colored, irradiated, fumigated, packaged, and shipped.

None of these processes enhances food quality but merely enables distribution over great distances and helps increase shelf life.[33]

Industrial agriculture has created the absurd situation whereby "[b]etween production, processing, distribution, and preparation, 10 calories of energy are required to create just one calorie of food energy."[34]

Indeed, its ability to combine productivity and ecological stability constitutes a key dimension of superiority of peasant or small-scale agriculture over industrial agriculture. A detailed but simple explanation of this is given by Tony Weis:

> Increased mechanization goes hand in hand with monocultures, which leave bare ground between planted rows. Conversely, small farms tend to make more intensive use of such space by cropping patterns that integrate complementary plant species . . . as well as integrating small livestock populations and using ecologically benign animal draught. Denser multicropped patterns that are frequently rotated, occasionally fallowed and integrated with small livestock and draught animal populations foster decomposition-assisting soil micro-organisms, detritivores, and invertebrates, which enhance the biological regulation of soil fertility, pests, weeds, and disease cycles with fewer chemicals and fertilizers than monocultures. This ability to renew and even enhance soils over time is also a function of the radically different time scales of farm management: because small farms are often drawing on knowledge passed down through generations on the land, they tend to be organized with a much longer-term objective of equilibrium, in contrast with how industrial monocultures are governed by an annual balance sheet.[35]

The sense that peasant and smallholder agriculture are backward stems from a series of assumptions that have little grounding in reality. According to Jan Douwe van der Ploeg, there are three related "mystifications" about peasant production. One is that there is a "technical ceiling" beyond which peasant production cannot go. A second is the operation of the so-called law of diminishing returns to labor-intensive peasant production. A third is the assumed stagnation of peasant production. Van der Ploeg argues that there is scant evidence for all three. In fact, he notes, Dutch agriculture became a leader in production globally in the period 1850 to 1956, when the numbers of small farmers grew in absolute terms, labor-intensive methods were dominant, capitalist or entrepreneurial farms disappeared, and there was a movement towards "repeasantization."[36]

Van der Ploeg notes that the logic of the peasant mode of production is different from capitalist logic, and the technological challenge is to build on the elements of the peasant model rather than supplant them with technology associated with capitalism. These elements are:

- Building upon and internalizing nature; coproduction and coevolution are central
- Distancing from markets on the input side; differentiation on the output side (low degree of commoditization)
- Centrality of craft and skill-oriented technologies
- Ongoing intensification based on quantity and quality of labor
- Multifunctionality
- Continuity of past, present, and future
- Increasing social wealth.[37]

There is progress in peasant agriculture, but it lies in a process where the use of technology is selective and not disruptive of the mode of production but is rather "in sync" with it. Technological development in peasant agriculture is not about standardizing production but building into the production process the capacity to deal with diversity. Technology is, in a very real sense, path dependent: its development takes different paths in different production paradigms. As van der Ploeg notes, in peasant farming,

> Technology is not only about linking artifacts and governing material flows—it is as much about interlinking people in specific ways in order to obtain the right kind of conditions and flows. Thus, skill is all about being able to overview, observe, handle, adjust, and coordinate extended domains of the social and natural world. This is done by building upon the specificities of different elements of the social and natural world. It is probably in this latter aspect (building on encountered and/or created specificities) that the main difference between skill-oriented and mechanical technologies resides. Continuous adjustments are neither feasible nor desirable. If you produce Coca-Cola, then only Coca-Cola comes out of your plant. A better or worse Coca-Cola is unthinkable and would be immediately perceived as a disaster. As objectified patterns of "through flow," mechanical technologies assume a standardized inflow, as much as they produce a standardized outflow. They cannot deal with specificity or variation. Specificity is a deviation, a threat and even potentially a destructive factor.[38]

Advanced science and peasant agriculture are not in contradiction. Incorporating science into small-scale farming is challenging but possible. According to Weis, "to significantly increase the scale of organic and near organic practices will require much more scientific research and training geared toward better understanding how agro-ecosystems operate and work and how key dynamics can be enhanced."[39] As an example, research into the functional complementaries of various insects can improve integrated pest management, while greater knowledge of soils and the dynamics of nutrient recycling can enlighten farmers on the best cropping patterns and rotations, nitrogen-fixing plants, and green manures to use to upgrade soil fertility.[40]

Other examples of how modern technologies can be blended with traditional patterns of agriculture are the raised farming beds in shallow lakes and marshes perfected by the Aztecs, transferred from the Mexico City suburbs to the lowland tropics of the country; the restoration, building, and improvement of Indian terraces in the Andes; and the discovery and rebuilding of a system of raised beds with canals that evolved on the high plains of the Peruvian Andes. In all cases, the harvest on the reconstructed fields compared favorably with that from conventional chemically fertilized soils.[41]

In the United States and other industrialized countries, one of the entrepreneurial successes of the last two decades has been organic agriculture, or production without pesticides and minimal or no petroleum-based fertilizers. With consciousness about the health hazards and negative environmental impacts of industrial agriculture spreading, the market for organic produce has become an extremely dynamic one. Small farmers and consumers have been connected through farmers' markets or through the creation of more permanent farmer-consumer networks. When they do not better or match in price the products of industrial agriculture, organic products more than offset the lower prices of corporate-produced commodities with their much less damaging health and environmental impacts.

Proponents of alternative agriculture, however, warn that if adopted as a technology alone, organic farming will face a losing battle, because any technology can only flourish in a supportive social and economic context. Miguel Altieri, a Via Campesina supporter, argues that if organic farming promotes the substitution of a biological agent for more toxic synthetic insecticides but leaves the monoculture structure of agriculture untouched, it is swimming against the tide:

> The acceptance of the present structure of agriculture as a given condition restricts the possibility of implementing alternatives that challenge such a structure. Thus, options for a diversified

agriculture are inhibited by, among other factors, the present trends in farm size and mechanization. Implementation of such mixed agriculture would only be possible as part of a broader program of land reform that includes land reform and machinery redesigned for polycultures. Merely introducing alternative agricultural designs will do little to change the underlying forces that led to monoculture production, farm size expansion, and large-scale mechanization in the first place.[42]

Altieri's warning is not about a potential problem but an urgent current threat, for corporate agriculture has increasingly "gone organic." With organic agriculture now being a $40 billion market in the United States, a number of supermarkets and corporations have acquired organic brands and small firms, set up partnerships with organic companies or have established their own organic lines. These firms include some major multinationals, such as Cadbury Schweppes, Coca-Cola, Danone, Deal, Heinz, Kellogg, Kraft, and Sara Lee. According to one report these paragons of industrial agriculture "increasingly dominate" the organic food sector.[43] Without actively battling corporate agriculture and without ensuring the social dimensions of alternative agriculture—small-scale production, family or communal ownership, community solidarity between farmers and consumers, short distance from farm to table—and focusing on technological issues alone, alternative agriculture is in danger of ending up a mere arm of industrial agriculture for a "niche market."

Articulating Food Sovereignty with Other Alternative Paradigms

Food sovereignty has elicited little acceptance outside of organizations focused on transformation of the agrifood system. This is probably because it hasn't articulated its implications for workers, industry, services, and other sectors of the economy.

Insofar as the urban population figures in the paradigm, it is mainly as consumers to be integrated into farmers' markets and as practitioners of urban gardening. Yet articulating the food sovereignty approach with other broader approaches that stress the same principles of small size, subsidiarity, diversity, equality, and democracy should, in theory, be faced with no insuperable difficulties. As some writers have noted, the food sovereignty approach, in fact, resonates with the paradigm of deglobalization identified with Focus on the Global South, a close ally of Via Campesina.[44]

According to Focus, deglobalization is not about withdrawing from the international economy. It is about making participation in the international economy one that builds local economic capacity rather than destroying it, as neoliberal trade policies do. Deglobalizaton would entail:

- making production for the domestic market, rather than production for export, the center of gravity for agriculture;
- enshrining the principle of subsidiarity in economic life by encouraging production of goods at the level of the community and at the national level if this can be done at reasonable cost to preserve community;
- using trade policy to protect local agriculture from destruction by dumped corporate-subsidized commodities with artificially low prices;
- using industrial policy to revitalize and strengthen the manufacturing sector;
- carrying out the long-postponed measures of income redistribution and land redistribution (including urban land reform) to create a vibrant internal market that would serve as the anchor of the economy and create local financial resources for investment;
- deemphasizing growth, emphasizing upgrading the quality of life, and maximizing equity to reduce environmental disequilibrium;

- not leaving strategic economic decisions to the market or to technocrats but to expand the scope of democratic decision making in the economy, so that all vital questions—such as which industries to develop or phase out, what proportion of the government budget to devote to agriculture, etc.— become subject to democratic choice;
- subjecting the private sector and the state to constant monitoring and supervision by civil society;
- transforming the property complex into a "mixed economy" that includes community cooperatives, private enterprises, and state enterprises, and excludes transnational corporations;
- encouraging the development and diffusion of environmentally congenial technology in both agriculture and industry.[45]

In both the food sovereignty paradigm and deglobalization, the aim is to move beyond the economics of narrow efficiency, in which the key criterion is the reduction of unit cost, never mind the social and ecological destabilization (considered "externalities") this process brings about. An effective economics, rather, strengthens social solidarity by subordinating the operations of the market to the values of equity, justice, and community by enlarging the sphere of democratic decision making. To use the language of Karl Polanyi, what food sovereignty and deglobalization are all about is "reembedding" the economy in society, instead of having society driven by the economy.

Another key point shared by the food sovereignty and deglobalization paradigms is the conviction that generalization of a one-size-fits-all model like neoliberalism or centralized socialism has been dysfunctional and destabilizing. Instead, diversity should be expected and encouraged, as it is in nature. This is not to say that there are no shared principles of alternative economics. There are, and indeed, they have already substantially emerged in the struggle against and critical reflection over the failure of both centralized socialism and neoliberalism. However, how these principles are concretely articulated will depend on the values, rhythms, and strategic choices of each society.

With the unraveling of global finance and the consequent collapse of the integrated global economy that is the legacy of the neoliberal era, paradigms such as food sovereignty and deglobalization have become acutely relevant to a world disillusioned with neoliberalism and capitalism and desperately looking for alternatives.

Farmers and peasants have long fed their local and national communities. Capitalism, especially in its neoliberal form, worked to consign them to the dustbin of history, replacing them with capital intensive monoculture geared mainly to a global supermarket of elite and middle-class consumers. In its goal of completely transforming the world's system of food production and distribution, one of the rationales advanced by industrial agriculture for the displacement of peasants and small farmers is that they do not have the capacity of feed the world. In fact, small farmers and peasants do not have ambitions of feeding the world, their horizons being limited to providing food for their local and national communities. It is by providing sustenance as best they can to their communities that peasants and farmers everywhere can be said to feed the world. And, despite the claims of its representatives that corporate agriculture is best at feeding the world, the creation of global production chains and global supermarkets, driven by the search for monopoly profits, has been accompanied by greater hunger, worse food, and greater agriculture-related environmental destabilization all around than at any other time in history.

Peasants and small farmers, however, are resilient, and at this time of global crisis, they present a vision of autonomy, diversity, and cooperation that may just be the key elements of a necessary social and economic reorganization. As environmental crises multiply, the social dysfunctions of urban industrialism accmulate, and globalization drags the world to a global depression, the "peasant's path" has increasing relevance to broad numbers of people beyond the countryside. Indeed, one finds movements of repeasantization, as entrepreneurial farmers abandon capitalist farming and increasing numbers of urbanites take up small-scale agriculture. One might even consider the possibility that, as van der Ploeg puts it, "the emergence of urban agriculture in many parts of the world signals the emergence of new numbers of (part-time) peasants and a simultaneous spatial shift of the peasantry from the countryside toward the big metropolises of the world."[46]

Conclusion

In recent years, one of the most dynamic sources of resistance to corporate-driven globalization has been the international movement of small farmers and peasants. The movement is endowed with attractive leaders and mass organizations like the MST that have captured the imagination and elicited the support of diverse sectors of global civil society.

The movement works to build coalitions with other networks and sectors of the global justice movement. This drive rests, in the case of Via Campesina, on the belief that small farmers and peasants can only successfully combat their condition of marginalization if they participate in broader movements for global transformation.

While resistance to such institutions as the WTO has been a hallmark of the movement, it has also taken seriously the challenge to articulate an alternative to the current agrifood system. The paradigm of food sovereignty challenges at every point the pillars of capitalist industrial agriculture, emphasizing, among other principles, food self-sufficiency, the right of a people to determine their patterns of agricultural production, farming that is not based on chemical-intensive agriculture or biotechnology, equality in land distribution, and agricultural production and distribution resting mainly on small farms and cooperative enterprises.

The movement valorizes traditional modes of production, seeing them as containing a great deal of wisdom from centuries of benign interaction with the biosphere. This attitude is not, however, a romanticization of the past, and many proponents of peasant agriculture are pursuing a symbiotic relationship between advanced science and small-scale, peasant farming that builds on the latter instead of destroying it. When they consider the environmental destabilization, health hazards, and low-quality products that come with capitalist industrial agriculture, partisans of small-scale agriculture are convinced of its superiority.

With the collapse of the global economy and with the deglobalization of production moving very fast, small farmer or peasant-based farming is becoming a model for the locally or regionally sustained alternative economies that people are searching for. Peasants and their allies are demonstrating how food sovereignty and other paradigms based on the same principles are relevant, and indeed crucial considerations for all sectors of society.

Notes

Introduction

1 United Nations, *World Economic Situation and Prospects 2009* (New York: United Nations, 2009), pp. 7–8.

2 Food and Agriculture Organization (FAO), "Briefing Paper: Hunger on the Rise" (September 17, 2008), (New York: United Nations), p. ix.

3 "Food costs spark protest in Senegal," April 27, 2008. http://english.aljazeera.net/news/africa/2008/04/200861423 3848478410.html.

4 Reed Lindsay, "Inside Haiti's Food Riots," *Al Jazeera*, April 16, 2008. http://english.aljazeera.net/news/americas/2008/04/ 200861517053857583.html.

5 United Nations, *World Economic Situation and Prospects 2009*, p. 46.

6 Peter Wahl, "Food Speculation: The Main Factor of the Price Bubble in 2008," (Berlin: WEED, 2009).

7 United Nations, *World Economic Situation and Prospects 2009*, p. 48.

8 Ibid.

9 FAO "Briefing paper: Hunger on the Rise."

10 Ibid., p. 26.

11 Gerardo Otero and Gabriela Pechlaner, "Latin American Agriculture, Food, and Biotechnology: Temperate Dietary Pattern Adoption and Unsustainability," in Gerardo Otero, ed., *Food for the Few: Neoliberal Globalism and Biotechnology Revolution in Latin America* (Austin: University of Texas Press, 2008), p. 50.

12 Lim Li Ching, "A New Green Revolution," *Development,* vol. 51, no. 4 (December 2008), p. 572. The IAASTD is the equivalent in the agricultural sciences of the Intergovernmental Panel on Climate Change on global warming issues.

13 Paul Collier, "The Politics of Hunger: How Illusion and Greed

Fan the Food Crisis," *Foreign Affairs,* vol. 87, no. 6 (November–December 2008), p. 73.

14 Ibid., p. 71.

15 Ibid.

16 "World Bank Neglects African Farming, Study Says," *New York Times,* October 15, 2007.

17 Eric Hobsbawm, *The Age of Extremes: The Short Twentieth Century, 1914–1991* (London: Abacus, 1994), p. 289.

18 Ibid., p. 291.

19 Deborah Bryceson, "Disappearing Peasantries? Rural Labor Redundancy in the Neo-liberal Era and Beyond," in Bryceson, C. Kay, and J. Mooij, eds., *Disappearing Peasantries* (London: Intermediate Technology Publications, 2000), p. 313.

20 *101 East, Al Jazeera,* December 19, 2008.

21 Frances Moore Lappé and Joseph Collins, "Why Can't People Feed Themselves?" in Douglas Boucher, ed., *The Paradox of Plenty* (Oakland: Food First, 1999), p. 65.

22 Jan Douwe van der Ploeg, *The New Peasantries* (London: Earthscan, 2008), p. 276.

23 Henry Bernstein, "Agrarian Questions from Transition to Globalization," in A. Haroon Akram-Lodhi and Cristobal Kay (New York: Routledge, 2009), p. 255.

24 Wayne Roberts, cited in Philip McMichael, "Food Sovereignty in Movement: The Challenge to Neo-liberal Globalization," draft, Cornell University, 2008.

25 Miguel Altieri, "Small Farms as a Planetary Ecological Asset: Five Key Reasons Why We Should Support the Revitalization of Small Farms in the Global South," Food First, 2008. http://www.foodfirst.org/en/node/2115.

Chapter 1   Capitalism Versus the Peasant

1 Barrington Moore, *The Social Origins of Dictatorship and Democracy: Lord and Peasant in the Making of the Modern World* (Boston: Beacon Press, 1966), p. 25.

2 Ibid., pp. 28–29.

3 Ellen Meiksins Wood, "The Agrarian Origins of Capitalism," in Fred Magdoff, John Bellamy Foster, and Frederick Buttle, *Hungry for Profit* (New York: Monthly Review Press, 2000), pp. 39–40.

4 Eric Hobsbawm, *Age of Extremes: The Short Twentieth Century* (London: Abacus, 1994), p. 289.

5 Moore, *The Social Origins of Dictatorship and Democracy*, p. 48.

6 Immanuel Wallerstein, *The Modern World-System,* Vol. 2 (New York: Academic Press, 1980), p. 201.

7 Nola Reinhardt and Peggy Barlett, "The Persistence of Family Farms in US Agriculture," *Sociologia Ruralis,* vol. 29, nos. 3–4 (1989), pp. 203–225.

8 Harriet Friedmann and Philip McMichael, "Agriculture and the State System: the Rise and Fall of National Agricultures, 1870 to the Present," *Sociological Ruralis,* vol. 29 (1989), pp. 93–117.

9 Ibid., pp. 97–98.

10 Clifford Geertz, *Agricultural Involution: The Process of Ecological Change in Indonesia* (Berkeley: University of California Press, 1963).

11 Clifford Geertz, quoted in Richard Robison, *Indonesia: the Rise of Capital* (North Sydney: Allen and Unwin, 1986), p. 16.

12 Amiya Kumar Bagchi, "Nineteenth Century Imperialism and Structural Transformation in Colonized Countries," in A. Haroon Akram-Lodhi and Cristobal Kay, *Peasants and Globalization: Political Economy, Rural Transformation, and the Agrarian Question* (New York: Routledge, 2009), p. 99.

13 John Ruggie, "International Regimes, Transactions, and Change: Embedded Liberalism in the Postwar Economic Order," *International Organization,* vol. 36, pp. 379–415.

14 Friedmann and McMichael, p. 105.

15 Bob Young, "Contribution to Debate on US Agricultural Policy," Cato Institute, Washington, DC, April 27, 2007. http://www.freetrade.org/node/618.

16 Reinhardt and Barlett, "The Persistance of Family Farms in US Agriculture," p. 216.

17 Eric Wolf, *Peasant Wars of the Twentieth Century* (New York: Harper and Row, 1969), p. 280.

18 Ibid., p. 105

19 In Chile, the agrarian reform program of the Christian Democrats (1964–70) led to the more radical program of the Popular Unity government led by Salvador Allende (1970–73).

20 Robert McNamara, *1974 Address to Board of Governors* (Washington, DC: World Bank, 1974), pp. 2–3.

21 World Bank, *Rural Development: Sector Working Paper* (Washington, DC: World Bank, 1975), p. 40.

22 Robert Ayres, "Breaking the Bank," *Foreign Policy,* no. 43, Summer 1981, pp. 111–112.

23 Farshad Araghi, "The Invisible Hand and the Visible Foot," in Akram-Lodhi and Kay, *Peasants and Globalization,* p. 133.

24 *Ibid.*

25 Harriet Friedmann, "Distance and Durability: Shaky Foundations

of the World Food Economy," in Philip McMichael, ed., *The Global Restructuring of Agro-Food Systems* (Ithaca: Cornell University Press, 1994), pp. 258–276.

26 Ibid., p. 272.

27 R. C. Lewontin, "The Maturing of Capitalist Agriculture: Farmer as Proletarian," in Fred Magdoff et al., *Hungry for Profit*, pp. 105–106.

28 Philip McMichael, "Global Food Politics," in Fred Magdoff et al., *Hungry for Profit*, p. 136.

29 Daniel Griswold, Contribution to debate on US Agricultural Policy, Cato Institute, Washington, DC., April 20, 2007. http://www.freetrade.org/node/618.

30 Deborah Bryceson, "Disappearing Peasantries? Rural Labor Redundancy in the Neo-Liberal Era and Beyond," in Bryceson, Cristobal Kay, and Jos Mooij, eds., *Disappearing Peasantries? Rural Labor in Africa, Asia, and Latin America* (London: Intermediate Technology Publications, 2000), p. 304–305; cited in Mike Davis, *Planet of Slums* (London: Verso, 2006), p. 15.

31 Utsa Patnaik, "External Trade, Domestic Employment, and Food Security: Recent Outcomes of Trade Liberalization and Neo-Liberal Economic Reforms in India," Paper presented at the International Workshop on Policies against Hunger III, Berlin, Oct. 20–22, 2004.

32 *The Hindu*, Nov. 12, 2007. http://www.hindu.com/2007/11/12/stories/2007111257790100.htm.

33 Vandana Shiva, "The Suicide Economy," ZNet, April 2004. http://www.countercurrents.org/glo-shiva050404.htm.

34 Daniel Imhoff, "Community Supported Agriculture," in Jerry Mander and Edward Goldsmith, eds., *The Case Against the Global Economy* (San Francisco: Sierra Club, 1996), p. 428.

35 "Turning Their Backs on the World," *Economist,* Feb. 21–27, 2009, p. 59. The author's book that the *Economist* refers to is Walden Bello, *Deglobalization: Ideas for a New World Economy* (London: Zed Press, 2002).

36 Ibid., p. 61.

Chapter 2   Eroding the Mexican Countryside

1 Ana de Ita, "Fourteen Years of NAFTA and the Tortilla Crisis," America Program, Center for International Policy, January 10, 2008. http://americas.irc-online.org/am/4879.

2 Morris Miller, *Debt and the Environment: Converging Crisis* (New York: UN, 1991), p. 215.

3 Walden Bello, Shea Cunningham, and Bill Rau, *Dark Victory: The United States, Structural Adjustment, and Global Poverty* (San Francisco: Food First, 1994), p. 39.

4 Damian Fraser, "Mexico Turns to Import Curbs as Deficit Grows," *Financial Times,* April 28, 1993.

5 Ricardo Grinspun and Maxwell Cameron, "Mexico: The Wages of Trade," *Report on the Americas,* vol. XXVI, no. 4 (February 1993), p. 34.

6 Ibid., p. 35.

7 Ibid.

8 Quoted in Carlos Heredia and Mary Purcell, "Structural Adjustment and the Polarization of Mexican Society," in Jerry Mander and Edward Goldsmith, eds., *The Case Against the Global Economy* (San Francisco: Sierra Club Books, 1996), p. 277.

9 Ibid.

10 Inter-American Development Bank, *Economic and Social Progress in Latin America 1991* (Washington, DC: Inter-American Development Bank, 1991), p. 124.

11 Inter-American Development Bank, *Economic and Social Progress in Latin America 1992* (Washington, DC: Inter-American Development Bank, 1992), p. 134.

12 Grinspun and Cameron, "Mexico: The Wages of Trade," p. 37.

13 Heredia and Purcell, "Structural Adjustment and the Polarization of Mexican Society," p. 278.

14 Robert Rubin and Jacob Weisberg, *In an Uncertain World* (New York: Random House, 2003), p. 6.

15 George Soros, *On Globalization* (New York: Public Affairs, 2002), p. 118.

16 Magdalena Barros-Nock, "The Mexican Peasantry and the *Ejido* in the Neo-Liberal Period," in Deborah Bryceson, Cristobal Kay, and Jos Mooij, eds., *Disappearing Peasantries: Rural Labor in Africa, Asia, and Latin America* (London: Intermediate Technology Publications, 2000), p. 168.

17 Quoted in Peter Rosset, *Food Is Different* (London: Zed Books, 2006), p. 55.

18 Ibid., p. 168.

19 Ibid.

20 Ibid, p. 56.

21 Ibid., p. 60.

22 For a comprehensive treatment of the role of speculation by the transnational middlemen in the "tortilla crisis," see Ana de Ita, "Fourteen Years of NAFTA and the Tortilla Crisis," Americas

Program, Center for International Policy, January 10, 2008. http://americas.irc-online.org/am/4879.

23 Horacio Mackinlay and Gerardo Otero, "State Corporatism and Peasant Organizations: Towards New Institutional Arrangements," in Gerardo Otero, ed., *Mexico in Transition* (London: Zed, 2004), p. 79.

24 Ibid., p. 79.

25 Deborah Bryceson, "Disappearing Peasantries? Rural Labor Redundancy in the Neo-Liberal Era and Beyond," in Bryceson, Kay, and Mooij, *Disappearing Peasantries,* p. 312.

26 Ibid.

27 Armando Bartra, "Rebellious Cornfield: Towards Food and Labor Self-Sufficiency," in Otero, *Mexico in Transition,* p. 23.

28 Ana de Ita, "Land Concentration in Mexico after PROCEDE," in Peter Rosset, Raj Patel, and Michael Courville, *Promised Land* (Oakland: Food First, 2006), p. 150.

29 Ibid., p.153.

30 Ibid., p. 158.

31 M. Conroy, D. Murray, and P. Rosset, *A Cautionary Tale: Failed US Development Policy in Latin America* (Boulder: Lynn Reiner, 1996).

32 Barros-Nock, "The Mexican Peasantry and The *Ejido* in the Neo-Liberal Period," p. 170.

33 R. Tuiran, C. Fuentes, and L. F. Ramos, "Dinamica Reciente de la Migracion Mexico-EU," *El Mercado de Valores,* Vol. 61, no. 8 (2001); cited in Raul Delgado Wise, "Labor and Migration Policies under Vicente Fox: Subordination to US Economic and Geopolitical Interests," in Otero, *Mexico in Transition,* p. 144.

34 Carolyn Lochhead, "Give and Take Across the Border," *San Francisco Chronicle,* May 21, 2006. http://www.sfgate.com/cgi-bin/article.cgi?file=/c/a/2006/05/21/MNGFQIVNAF1.DTL.

35 Laura Carlsen, "The Mexican Farmers' Movement: Exposing the Myths of Free Trade" (Mexico City: Interhemispheric Resource Center, 2003), quoted in Rosset, pp. 58–59.

36 Lochhead, "Give and Take Across the Border."

37 E-mail communication, April 30, 2008.

Chapter 3   Creating a Rice Crisis in the Philippines

1 Untitled study attributed to Dale Hill, agricultural loan officer for the Philippines, World Bank, Washington, DC, undated, p. 159.

2 Ibid., p. 84.

3 World Bank, "Poverty, Basic Needs, and Employment: A Review and Assessment," confidential first draft, World Bank, Washington, DC, January 1980, p. 212.

4 Conrad Carino, "Rice Crisis 'Imminent' Long Ago," *Manila Times,* April 6, 2008. http://www.manilatimes.net/national/2008/apr/06/yehey/top_stories/20080406top3.html.

5 Charles Lindsay, "The Political Economy of Economic Policy Reform in the Philippines," in Andrew MacIntyre and Kanishka Jayasuriya, eds., *The Dynamics of Economic Policy Reform in the Philippines* (Singapore: Oxford University Press, 1992).

6 Eric Boras, "Government Loses P120 Billion to Tariff Cuts," *Business World,* October 20, 2003.

7 World Bank, *World Bank Debt Tables, Vol. 2* (Washington, DC: World Bank, 1994), p. 378.

8 Ibid., p. 379.

9 World Bank, *World Development Indicators 1998* (Washington, DC: World Bank, 1997), p. 199.

10 Ibid., p. 131.

11 Florian Alburo, et al., "Towards Recovery and Sustainable Growth," School of Economics, University of the Philippines, Diliman, Quezon City, September 1985.

12 Calculated from figures provided in World Bank, *Accelerating Inclusive Growth and Deepening Fiscal Stability* (Draft Report for the Philippine Development Forum 2008) (Manila: World Bank, 2008).

13 Emmanuel de Dios et al., "The Deepening Crisis: The Real Score on Deficits and the Public Debt," Faculty of Economics, University of the Philippines, August 2004.

14 World Bank, *Accelerating Inclusive Growth,* p. 5.

15 Ibid., p. 27.

16 Ibid.

17 Government data from Riza Bernabe, personal communication, May 5, 2008.

18 Wilfredo Cruz and Robert Repetto, *The Environmental Effects of Stabilization and Structural Adjustment* (Washington, DC: World Resources Insitute, 1992), p. 48.

19 Rovik Obanil, "Rice Safety Nets Act: More of a Burden Than a Shield," *Farm News and Views* (1st Quarter 2002), p. 10.

20 *Selected Agricultural Statistics, 1998 and 2002* (Quezon City: Department of Agriculture, 1998, 2002); Rovik Obanil, "Rice Safety Nets Act," p.10.

21 Aileen Kwa, "A Guide to the WTO's Doha Work Program: The

'Development' Agenda Undermines Development," Focus on the Global South, Bangkok, January 2003.

22 *Selected Agricultural Statistics, 1998 and 2002* (Quezon City: Department of Agriculture, 1998, 2002).

23 See Walden Bello et al., *The Anti-Development State: The Political Economy of Permanent Crisis in the Philippines* (Quezon City: University of the Philippines, 2004), pp. 146–148.

24 *Selected Agricultural Statistics 1998 and 2002* (Quezon City: Department of Agriculture, 1998, 2002).

25 Submission of Republic of the Philippines, World Trade Organization Committee on Agriculture, Geneva, July 1, 2003.

26 Figures from World Bank, Bureau of Customs and National Statistical Coordination Board.

27 Figures from World Bank, *World Development Indicators 1998*, p. 227 and *World Development Indicators 2003*, p. 235.

28 Cited in Boras, "Government Loses P120 Billion to Tariff Cuts."

29 Solita Monsod, "Contempt for Farmers," *Business World*, December 4, 2008, p. 4.

30 Ricardo Arlanza, Prudenciano Gordoncillo, Hans Meliczek, Juan Palafox, and Linda Penalba, "Study on Post-LAD Scenarios," Department of Agrarian Reform and German Technical Cooperation (GTZ), Manila, April 2006, p. 11.

31 World Bank, *Accelerating Inclusive Growth and Deepening Fiscal Stability*, p. 82.

32 Ibid., pp. 79–80.

33 A. Haroon Akram-Lodhi, Cristobal Kay, and Saturnino Borras Jr., "The Political Economy of Land and the Agrarian Question in an Era of Neoliberal Globalization," in A. Haroon Akram-Lodhi and Cristobal Kay, ed., *Peasants and Globalization: Political Economy, Rural Transformation, and the Agrarian Question* (Abingdon: Routledge, 2009), p. 231; see also Saturnino Borras Jr., *Competing Views and Strategies on Agrarian Reform, Vol. I: International Perspectives* (Quezon City: Ateneo de Manila University Press, 2008), p. 81–107; and *Vol. II: Philippine Perspective* (Quezon City: Ateneo de Manila University Press, 2009), pp. 72–106.

34 Mary Ann Manahan, "The Battle for CARP Extension and Meaningful Reforms," in Aya Fabros, ed., *Focus on the Philippines 2008 Yearbook* (Quezon City: Focus on the Global South, 2008), p. 229.

35 James Putzel, foreword to Borras, *Competing Views and Strategies on Agrarian Reform, Vol. II*, p. xi.

Chapter 4   Destroying African Agriculture

1 "Africa's Hunger—A Systemic Crisis," *BBC News,* January 21, 2006. http://news.bbc.co.uk/2/hi/africa/462232.stm.

2 "The Development of African Agriculture." http://www. africangreenrevolution.com/cgi-bin/african_green_rev/printer_ friendly.cgi?f.

3 See, *inter alia,* Oxfam International, *Causing Hunger: An Overview of the Food Crisis in Africa* (Oxford: Oxfam, July 2006).

4 United Nations, *World Economic Situation and Prospects* (New York: United Nations, 2009), p. 26.

5 Deborah Bryceson, "African Peasants' Centrality and Marginality: Rural Labour Transformations," in Deborah Bryceson, Cristobal Kay, and Jos Mooij, eds., *Disappearing Peasantries? Rural Labour in Africa, Asia, and Latin America* (London: Intermediate Technology Publications, 2000), p. 49.

6 Philip Raikes, "Modernization and Adjustment in Peasant Agriculture," in Bryceson et al., eds., *Disappearing Peasantries,* p. 74.

7 Bryceson, p. 50.

8 Kjell Havnevik, Deborah Bryceson, Lars-Erik Birgegard, Prosper Matondi, and Atakilte Beyene, "African Agriculture and the World Bank," *Pambazuka News,* March 11, 2008. http://www. pambazuka.org/en/category/features/46564.

9 Benno Ndulu, *Challenges of African Growth* (Washington, DC: World Bank, 2007), p. 10.

10 Ngaire Woods, *The Globalizers* (Ithaca, NY: Cornell University Press, 2006), p. 144.

11 Devesh Kapur, John Lewis, and Richard Webb, *The World Bank: Its First Half Century* (Washington, DC: Brookings Institute, 1997); cited in ibid.

12 Raikes, "Modernization and Adjustment in Peasant Agriculture," pp. 74–75.

13 Walden Bello, Shea Cunningham, and Bill Rau, *Dark Victory: The United States, Structural Adjustment, and Global Poverty* (London: Pluto Press, 1994), pp. 36–37.

14 Jose Maria Fanelli, Roberto Frenkel, and Lance Taylor, "The World Development Report 1991: A Critical Assessment," in *International Monetary and Financial Issues for the 1990s* (New York: United Nations Conference on Trade and Development, 1992), p. 19.

15 Ibid., p.14.

16 Samuel Wangwe and Haji Semboja, "Impact of Structural

Adjustment on Industrialization and Technology in Africa," in Thandika Mkwandire and Charles Soludo, eds., *African Voices on Structural Adjustment* (Dakar: CODESRIA, 2003), p. 173.

17 Ibid.

18 Alice Amsden and Rolph Van der Hoeven, "Manufacturing Output and Wages in the 1980s: Labor's Loss toward Century's End," paper prepared for the Conference on Sustainable Development with Equity in the 1990s, Global Studies Program, University of Wisconsin, Madison, May 13–16, 1993, pp. 18–19.

19 Wangwe and Semboja, "Impact of Structural Adjustment," p. 179.

20 Peter Robinson and Somsak Tambunlertchai, "Africa and Asia: Can High Rates of Growth Be Replicated?" *Occasional Papers, International Center for Economic Growth*, no. 40 (1993), p. 13.

21 Indeed, many studies have shown a positive relationship between public investment and private investment. One key study of a panel of developing economies from 1980 to 1997 found that public investment complemented private investment, and that, on average, a 10 percent increase in public investment was associated with a 2 percent increase in private investment. Lufti Erden and Randall Holcombe, "The Effects of Public Investment on Private Investment in Developing Economies," *Public Finance Review,* vol. 33, no. 5 (2005), pp. 575–602.

22 Oxfam, *Causing Hunger,* p. 18.

23 "The New Face of Hunger," *Economist,* April 17, 2008. http://www.economist.com/world/internatiional/PrinterFriendly.cfm?story_id=11049284.

24 Charles Abugre, *Behind Crowded Shelves: As Assessment of Ghana's Structural Adjustment Experiences, 1983–1991* (San Francisco: Food First, 1993), p. 87.

25 Oxfam, *Causing Hunger,* p. 20.

26 See "Did the IMF Cause a Famine?," Yingsakfoodnetwork.com, April 28, 2008. http://www.yingsakfoodnetwork.com/did_the_imf.asp.

27 Havnevik et al, "African Agriculture and the World Bank."

28 Christopher Stevens and Jane Kennan, "Food Aid and Trade," in Stephen Devereaux and Simon Maxwell, eds., *Food Security in Sub-Saharan Africa* (London: ITDG Publishing, 2001), pp. 174–175.

29 Ibid., p. 176.

30 Peter Rosset, *Food Is Different: Why We Must Get the WTO Out of Agriculture* (London: Zed, 2006), p. 66.

31 "Trade Talks Round Going Nowhere sans Progress in Farm Reform," *Business World,* Sept. 8, 2003, p. 15.

32 Rosset, *Food Is Different*, p. 66.

33 Quoted in "Cakes and Caviar: The Dunkel Draft and Third World Agriculture," *Ecologist,* vol. 23, no. 6 (November–December 1993), p. 220.

34 OECD Agricultural Trade Statistics, http://www.oecd.org/dataoecd/48/2/40010981.xls.

35 Oxfam International, *Rigged Rules and Double Standards* (Oxford: Oxfam International, 2002), p. 112.

36 Ibid., p. 13.

37 Quoted in Miller, *Debt and the Environment*, p. 70.

38 Ngaire Woods, *The Globalizers: The IMF, the World Bank, and Their Borrowers* (Ithaca, NY: Cornell University Press, 2006), p. 158.

39 Stephanie Nolen, "How Malawi Went from a Nation of Famine to a Nation of Feast," *Globe and Mail,* October 12, 2007; "Starter Packs: A Strategy to Fight Hunger in Developing Countries: Lessons from Malawi," *CAB Abstracts,* http://www.cababstractsplus.org/google/abstract.asp?aspAcNo=20053142997.

40 Ibid.

41 Ibid.

42 IMF statement, quoted in "Famine in Malawi Exposes IMF Negligence," *Economic Justice News,* vol. 5, no. 2 (June 2002), http://www.50years.org/cms/ejn/story/89. This article summarizes a report by ActionAid, *State of Disaster: Causes, Consequences, and Policy Lessons from Malawi,* released on June 13, 2002.

43 FAO Representation Office, "Briefing File for Director-General Visit to Malawi," Lilongwe, November 27–29, 2008, p. 3.

44 World Bank Country Director Tim Gilbo, quoted in Nolen "How Malawi Went from a Nation of Famine to a Nation of Feast".

45 Department for International Development (DFID), "A Record Harvest in Malawi," *Case Studies,* May 8, 2007. http://www.dfid.gov.uk/casestudies/files/africa%5Cmalawi-harvest.asp.

46 Cited in FAO, "Briefing File," Lilongwe, November 27, 2008.

47 Joachim von Braun, "Rising Food Prices: What Should be Done?" *IFPRI Policy Brief,* April 2008. http://www.ifpri.org.

48 See Abhijit Banerjee, Angus Deaton, Nora Lustig, and Ken Rogoff, "An Evaluation of World Bank Research, 1998–2005," http://econ.worldbank.org/WBSITE/EXTERNAL/EXTDEC/0,,content MDK:21165468~pagePK:64165401~piPK:64165026~theSite PK:469372,00.html.

49 Independent Evaluation Group (IEG), *World Bank Assistance to Agriculture in Sub-Saharan Africa* (Washington, DC: World Bank, 2007), p. 65.

50 Ibid., p. 67.
51 Ibid., pp. 67–68.
52 Ibid., p. 66.
53 Ibid., p. 67.
54 Ndulu, *Challenges of African Growth*, pp. 158, 159.
55 World Bank, *World Bank Development Report 2008: Agriculture for Development* (Washington, DC: World Bank, 2008), p. 138.
56 Havnevik et al., "African Agriculture and the World Bank."
57 Paul Collier, "The Politics of Hunger: How Illusion and Greed Fan the Food Crisis," *Foreign Affairs*, vol. 87, no. 6 (November–December 2008), p. 71.
58 In 2002, Zambia refused a US donation of genetically modified grain, and its neighbors agreed to accept GM grain only if it was milled before distribution. These countries were concerned that letting in food aid containing genetically modified material would lead to the planting of seeds and the contamination of domestic crops.
59 Havnevik et al., "African Agriculture and the World Bank."

Chapter 5   Peasants, the Party, and Agrarian Crisis in China

1 chinadialogue, June 3, 2008. http//www.chinadialogue.net.
2 Lester Brown, *Who Will Feed China? Wake-up Call for a Small Planet* (New York: W. W. Norton, 1995).
3 See United Nations, *World Economic Situation and Prospects 2009* (New York: United Nations, 2009), p. 48.
4 Bryan Lohmar and Fred Gale, "Who Will China Feed?" *Amber Waves*, June 2008. http://www.ers.usda.gov/AmberWaves/June08/Features/ChinaFeed.htm.
5 World Bank, *World Bank Development Report 2008* (Washington, DC: World Bank, 2008), p. 61.
6 Ibid.
7 Chunlai Chen and Ron Duncan, eds., *Agriculture and Food Security in China* (Canberra: ANU Press, 2008), p. 21.
8 Ibid., p. 83.
9 C. A. Carter and A. Estrin, "China's Trade Integration and Impacts on Factor Markets," mimeo, Department of Agricultural and Resource Economics, University of California, Davis, 2001.
10 Deepak Bhattasali, Shanton Li, and Will Martin, "Impacts and Policy Implications of WTO Accession for China," in Bhattasali, Li, and Martin, eds., *China and the WTO: Accession, Policy Reform,*

and Poverty Reduction Strategies (Washington, DC: World Bank, 2004), p. 224.

11 Dominique van der Mensbrugghe and John C. Beghin, "Global Agricultural Reform: What Is at Stake?" in M. Ataman Aksoy and John C. Beghin, *Global Agricultural Trade and Developing Countries* (Washington, DC: World Bank, 2005), p. 125.

12 Bhattasali et al., "Impacts and Policty Implications," p. 7.

13 Lohmar and Gale, "Who Will China Feed?"

14 C. Fred Bergsten, Bates Gill, Nicholas Lardy, and Derek Mitchell, *China: The Balance Sheet* (New York: Public Affairs, 2006), p. 55.

15 Food and Agriculture Organization, Regional Office for Asia and the Pacific (FAO-RAP), *Poverty Alleviation and Food Security in Asia: Lessons and Challenges* (Bangkok: FAO, 1998), Annex 3.

16 Liao Shaolian, "Food Production in China," in Aileen Baviera, Liao Shaolian, and Clarissa Militante, eds., *Food Security in China and Southeast Asia* (Quezon City: Philippine-China Development Resource Center, 1999), p. 15.

17 Lu Qi, Leif Soderlund, Wu Peilin, and Li Juan, "Cultivated Land Loss Arising from the Rapid Urbanization in China," *Agrifood Research Reports 68,* MTT Agrifood Research, Finland, undated

18 FAO-RAP, *Poverty Alleviation and Food Security.*

19 Jung Chang and Jon Halliday, *Mao: The Unknown Story* (New York: Random House, 2005), p. 427.

20 Ibid.

21 Chen Guidi and Wu Chantao, *Will the Boat Sink the Water?* (New York: Public Affairs, 2006), p. 148.

22 Roderick MacFarquhar and Michael Schoenhals, *Mao's Last Revolution* (Cambridge, MA: Harvard University Press, 2006), p. 271.

23 Ibid., p. 272.

24 Ibid.

25 Chen and Wu, *Will the Boat Sink the Water?,* p. 148.

26 Ashok Gulati, Shenggen Fan, and Sara Dalafi, *The Dragon and the Elephant: Agricultural and Rural Reforms in China and India,* MTID Discussion Paper no. 87, (Washington, DC: International Food Policy Research Institute, 2005), p. 15.

27 Minxin Pei, *China's Trapped Transition: The Limits of Developmental Autocracy* (Cambridge, MA: Harvard University Press, 2006), p. 26.

28 Chen and Wu, *Will the Boat Sink the Water?,* p. 149.

29 Ibid., pp. 151–152.

30 Pei, *China's Trapped Transition,* p. 193.

31 Bergsten et al., *China: The Balance Sheet,* p. 41.

32 Kathy Le Mons Walker, "From Covert to Overt: Everyday Peasant Politics in China and the Implications for Transnational Agrarian Movements," *Journal of Peasant Studies*, vol. 9, nos. 2 and 3 (April and July 2008), p. 472.
33 Bergsten et al., *China: The Balance Sheet*, p. 36.
34 Quoted in Walker, "From Covert to Overt," p. 466.
35 Ibid.
36 Ibid.
37 Cited in ibid., p. 467.
38 Chen and Wu, *Will the Boat Sink the Water?*, p. 187.
39 Bergsten et al., *China: The Balance Sheet*, pp. 40–41.
40 Pei, *China's Trapped Transition*, p. 194.
41 Chen and Wu, *Will the Boat Sink the Water?*, pp. 191–201.
42 Dennis Lynch, *Rising China and Asian Democratization* (Stanford: Stanford University Press, 2006), pp. 88–149.
43 Pei, *China's Trapped Transition*, p. 79.
44 Chen and Wu, *Will the Boat Sink the Water?*, p. 218.
45 Lohmar and Gale "Who Will China Feed?".
46 Central Committee, Communist Party of China, "Decision on Major Issues Concerning the Advancement of Rural Reform and Development," Beijing, October 2008. Translated by Tu Wen Wen.
47 Lu Zixiu, an expert on rural affairs, quoted in Antonaneta Bezlova, "Flirting with Land Tenure Reforms," *Inter-Press Service*, October 13, 2008.
48 "China Liberalizes Farmers' Land Use Right to Boost Rural Development," *Xinhua*, October 19, 2008. http://news.xinhuanet.com/english/2008-10/19/content_10218172.htm.

Chapter 6 Agrofuels and Food Insecurity

1 Aditya Chakrabortty, "Secret Report: Biofuels Caused Food Crisis," *The Guardian*, July 3, 2008. http://www.guardian.co.uk/environment/2008/jul/03/biofuels.renewableenergy.
2 Donald Mitchell, "A Note on Rising Food Prices," World Bank website, July 2008. http://go.worldbank.org/31PG0020G0.
3 Chakrabortty, "Secret Report: Biofuels Caused Food Crisis."
4 APEC biofuels website, July 21, 2008. http://www.biofuels.apec.org/me_united_states.html.
5 "Biofuels—At What Cost? Government support for ethanol and biodiesel in the United States: 2007 Update," Global Subsidies Initiative website, October 2007. http://www.globalsubsidies.org.
6 "US Biofuel Dumping," Change Alley website, March 2008.

http://environmentdebate.co.uk/2008/03/10/us-biofuel-dumping/.

7 Ibid.

8 Brenda Goodman, "Pollution Is Called a By-product of a 'Clean' Fuel," *The New York Times,* March 11, 2008. http://www.nytimes.com/2008/03/11/us/11biofuel.html?_r=2&page wanted=1&ei= 5070&en=ab929123583ae710&ex=1205899200&emc=eta1.

9 Cargill website, http://www.cargill.com/news/issues/palm_sustainability.htm.

10 Doug Cameron, "Cargill Chief in Warning over Biofuels Boom," *The Financial Times,* May 2007. http://www.ft.com/cms/s/0/ff76e900-0e4a-11dc-8219-000b5df10621.html?nclick_check=1.

11 Joseph Weber, "The Downside of ADM's Focus on Biofuels," *Business Week* website, December 2008; http://www.businessweek.com/magazine/content/09_02/b4115034744790.htm.

12 Ibid.

13 Dana Childs, "Chevron Pumps More Money into University Biofuel Research," Cleantech website, May 2007. http://cleantech.com/news/1233/chevron-pumps-more-money-into-universi.

14 "Corporate power—Agrofuels and the Expansion of Agribusiness," Grain website, July 2007. http://www.grain.org/seedling/?id=478.

15 Silvia Ribeiro and Hope Shand, "Seeding New Technologies to Fuel Old Injustices," *Development* 51(4), 2008, 496–505.

16 European Commission, *Biofuels Progress Report* (Brussels: European Commission, 2007).

17 Jasper van den Munckhof, "Linking Political Theory to Recent EU and US Policies on Biofuels: Realism and Liberal Institutionalism," *An Exercise in Worldmaking: The Institute of Social Studies Best Student Essays of 2005/06* (The Hague: Institute of Social Studies, 2006), pp. 94–103.

18 David Smith, "Five Years to Save the Orangutan," *The Guardian,* March 25, 2007. http://www.guardian.co.uk/environment/2007/mar/25/conservation.theobserver.

19 Jutta Kill, "Biofuels Are Not the Answer," Transnational Institute website, March 2007. http://www.tni.org/detail_page.phtml?act_id=16229.

20 Ibid.

21 Jackson West, "Vinod Khosla's Brazilian Ethanol Venture Uses Slave Labor, Just Like Most Valley Startups We Know," Valley Gawker website, March 28, 2008. http://valleywag.gawker .com/373570/

vinod-khoslas-brazilian-ethanol-venture-uses-slave-labor-just-like-most-valley-startups-we-know.

22 Ibid.

23 "Slave Labor Casts Pall over Brazil's Biofuels Conference," *The Financial Times Express*, November 19, 2008. http://www.thefinancialexpress-bd.info/search_index.php?page=detail news&news_id=51155.

24 Sabrina Valle, "Losing Forests to Fuel Cars," *Washington Post*, July 31, 2007. http://www.washingtonpost.com/wp-dyn/content/article/2007/07/30/AR2007073001484.html.

25 Ibid.

26 "US Ethanol may drive Amazon deforestation," Mongabay Website, May 17, 2007. http://news.mongabay.com/2007/0516-ethanol_amazon.html.

27 Association of Southeast Asian Nations Website, January 15, 2007. http://www.aseansec.org/19319.htm.

28 APEC Biofuels Website, July 21, 2008. http://www.biofuels.apec.org/me_united_states.html.

29 United Nations Economic Commission for Latin America and the Caribbean Press Release, November 18, 2008. http://www.eclac.org/cgi-bin/getProd.asp?xml=/prensa/noticias/comunicados/9/34559/P34559.xml&xsl=/prensa/tpl-i/p6f.xsl&base=/tpl-i/top-bottom.xsl.

30 *First High Level Biofuels Seminar in Africa Bulletin*, August 4, 2007; http://www.iisd.ca/africa/biofuels/html/arc0901e.html#Action Plan for Biofuels Development in Africa.

31 "Global trends driving 'land grab' in poor nations: activists," *AFP*, January 3, 2009. http://www.google.com/hostednews/afp/article/ALeqM5iAAAFho9FSMtNoh1BfnqWlgFT5LQ.

32 Richard Spencer, "South Korean company takes over part of Madagascar to grow biofuels," *Telegraph* Website, November 20, 2008. http://www.telegraph.co.uk/earth/agriculture/3487668/South-Korean-company-takes-over-part-of-Madagascar-to-grow-biofuels.html. There are reports that the new government that came to power in a coup in March 2009 has canceled the Daewoo contract owing to popular opposition. There is no certainty, however, that it will not be renegotiated.

33 "Global trends driving 'land grab' in poor nations: activists," *AFP*.

34 World Bank, *Accelerating Inclusive Growth and Deepening Fiscal Stability: Draft Report for the Philippines Development Forum 2008* (Manila: World Bank, 2008), p. 78.

35 "Rural Renewable Energy in the Greater Mekong Subregion,"

Asian Development Bank Website, 2008. http://www.adb.org/documents/brochures/gms-biofuel/gms-biofuel-brochure.pdf.
36 UN-Energy, Food and Agriculture Organization Website, April 2007. http://www.fao.org/docrep/010/a1094e/a1094e00.htm.
37 AFP Website, July 16, 2008. http://afp.google.com/article/ALeqM5iICJVgwhmr25fQlUuhV4edgcZ8Dw.
38 *Biofuels Support Policies: An Economic Assessment,* Organisation for Economic Co-operation and Development, 2008. Policy Brief.
39 Ed Gallagher, *The Gallagher Review of the Indirect Effects of Biofuel Production,* Renewable Fuels Agency, 2008, Report Commissioned by the UK Secretary of State Transport.
40 Ibid.
41 Andres Cala, "EU Rethinking Biofuels Usage," *Energy Tribune,* June 12, 2008. http://www.energytribune.com/articles.cfm?aid=920.
42 EurActiv Website, December 2, 2008. http://www.euractiv.com/en/transport/eu-lawmakers-split-biofuels/article-177398.
43 Gretchen Gordon, "The Global Free Market in Biofuels," *Development* 51 (2008), 481–487.
44 Danny Bradbury, "Texas labels biofuels targets 'bad public policy'," Business Green Website, August 11, 2008. http://www.businessgreen.com/business-green/news/2223632/texas-labels-biofuel-targets.
45 Eric Holt-Gimenez, "The Biofuels Myths," Food First Website, July 10, 2007. http://www.foodfirst.org/en/node/1716.
46 "Study: Ethanol production consumes six units of energy to produce just one," Science Daily Website, April 1, 2005. http://www.sciencedaily.com/releases/2005/03/050329132436.htm.

Chapter 7   Resistance and the Road to the Future

1 Interview with brother of Jeon Tae-Il, Seoul, May 20, 1988.
2 "Korean Peasant League," http://ijunnong.net/en/article/index.php?pl=2.
3 José Bové, "A Farmers' International?" *New Left Review* 12 (November–December 2001). http://www.newleftreview.org/A2358.
4 Brenda Baletti, Tamara Johnson, and Wendy Wolford, "Late Mobilization: Transnational Peasant Networks and Grassroots Organizing in Brazil and South Africa,"*Journal of Agrarian Change,* vol. 8, nos. 2 and 3 (April and July 2008), pp. 295–298.
5 João Pedro Stédile, "Landless Battalions: The Sem Terra Movement of Brazil," *New Left Review.* 15 (May–June 2002), p. 99.

6 Ibid.
7 Ibid., p. 100.
8 Ibid., p. 99.
9 Ibid.
10 Raj Patel, *Stuffed and Starved: Markets, Power, and the Hidden Battle for the World Food System* (London: Portobello Books, 2007), p. 211.
11 João Pedro Stédile, "The Class Struggles in Brazil: The Perspective of the MST," in Leo Panitch and Colin Leys, eds., *Socialist Register 2008* (London: Merlin Press, 2007), p. 280.
12 Isabella Kenfield, "Landless Rural Workers Confront Brazil's Lula," CENSA, June 18, 2007. http://www.tni.org/detail_page. phtml?act_id=17001.
13 Ibid.
14 Monica Dias Martins, "Learning to Participate: The MST Experience in Brazil," in Peter Rosset, Raj Patel, and Michael Courville, *Promised Land: Competing Visions of Agrarian Reform* (Oakland: Food First, 2006), p. 276.
15 Annette Desmarais, *La Via Campesina: Globalization and the Power of Peasants* (London: Pluto Press, 2007), pp. 92–103.
16 Paul Nicholson, "Via Campesina: Responding to Global Systemic Crisis," interview in *Development*, vol. 51, no. 4 (2008), p. 457.
17 Cited in Saturnino Borras Jr., Marc Edelman, and Cristobal Kay, "Transnational Agrarian Movements: Origins and Politics, Campaigns and Impacts," *Journal of Agrarian Change,* vol. 8, nos. 2 and 3, (April and July 2008), p. 172.
18 Saturnino Borras, "La Via Campesina and the Global Campaign for Agrarian Reform," *Journal of Agrarian Change*, vol. 8, nos. 2 and 3 (April and July 2008), p. 274.
19 Ibid., p. 273.
20 Edward Goldsmith, "The Last Word: Family, Community, Democracy," in Jerry Mander and Edward Goldsmith, eds., *The Case. Against the Global Economy* (San Francisco: Sierra Club, 1996), p. 313.
21 Ibid., p. 275.
22 Desmarais, *La Via Campesina,* p. 132.
23 Quoted in "Cakes and Caviar: The Dunkel Draft and Third World Agriculture," *Ecologist,* vol. 23, no. 6 (November–December 1993), p. 220.
24 Via Campesina, "Food Sovereignty and International Trade," Position paper approved at the Third International Conference of the Via Campesina, Bangalore, India, October 3–6, 2000. Cited in Desmarais, p. 34.
25 Quoted in Desmarais, *La Via Campesina.*

26 José Bové, "A Farmers' International?"

27 Peter Rosset, quoted in Philip McMichael, "Food Sovereignty in Movement: The Challenge to Neo-Liberal Globalization," draft, Cornell University, 2008.

28 Philip McMichael, "Food Sovereignty in Movement: The Challenge to Neo-Liberal Globalization."

29 Desmarais, *La Via Campesina*, p. 38.

30 Ibid., pp. 38–39.

31 Henry Bernstein, "Agrarian Questions from Transition to Globalization," in A. Haroon Akram-Lodhi and Cristobal Kay, eds., *Peasants and Globalization* (New York: Routledge, 2009), p. 255.

32 Miguel Altieri and Clara Nicholls, "Scaling up Agroecological Approaches for Food Sovereignty in Latin America," *Development*, vol. 51, no. 4 (December 2008), p. 474.

33 Daniel Imhoff, "Community Supported Agriculture," in Mander and Goldsmith, *The Case Against the Global Economy*, pp. 425–426.

34 Ibid., p. 426.

35 Tony Weis, *The Global Food Economy: The Battle for the Future of Farming* (London: Zed, 2007), p. 167.

36 Jan Douwe van der Ploeg, *The New Peasantries: Struggles for Autonomy and Sustainability in an Era of Globalization* (London: Earthscan, 2008), pp. 46–47.

37 Van der Ploeg, *The New Peasantries*, pp. 114–115

38 Ibid., p. 172.

39 Weis, *The Global Food Economy*, p. 170

40 Ibid.

41 Altieri and Nichols, "Scaling up Agroecological Approaches," pp. 476–477.

42 Miguel Altieri, "Ecological Impacts of Industrial Agriculture and the Possibilities for Truly Sustainable Farming," in Fred Magdoff, John Bellamy Foster, and Frederick Buttel, eds., *Hungry for Profits* (New York: Monthly Review Press, 2000), p. 89.

43 "The Battle for the Soul of the Organic Movement," *Briefing Room*, CNN, October 9, 2006; http://edition.cnn.com/2006/WORLD/europe/10/09/tbr.organic/.

44 See Borras, "La Vin Campesina," p. 260.

45 See Walden Bello, *Deglobalization: Ideas for a New World Economy* (London: Zed, 2004), pp. 112–114.

46 Van der Ploeg, *The New Peasantries*, p. 37.

Index

Figures in **bold** refer to charts.